Royal Tastes

Royal Tastes

Erotic Writings

Paul Verlaine

Translated with an Introduction
and Commentary by Alan Stone

Harmony Books, New York

Published by Harmony Books, a division of Crown Publishers,
Inc., One Park Avenue, New York, New York 10016 and
simultaneously in Canada by General Publishing Company
Limited

HARMONY and colophon are trademarks of Crown Publishers,
Inc.

An edition entitled *Women and Men* was published in a slightly
different form by The Stonehill Publishing Company in 1980.

Manufactured in the United States of America

Library of Congress Cataloging in Publication Data

Verlaine, Paul, 1844-1896.
  Royal tastes.

  Translation of: Oeuvres libres.
  1. Erotic poetry, French—Translations into English.
2. Erotic poetry, English—Translations from French.
3. Verlaine, Paul, 1844-1896—Translations, English.
I. Title.
PQ2463.A28 1984   841'.8   84-3824
ISBN 0-517-55495-X

10 9 8 7 6 5 4 3 2 1

First Revised Edition

CONTENTS

MEN

OEUVRES LIBRES

INTRODUCTION

Paul Verlaine (1844–1896), the poet of elusive music, of melancholy and nostalgia, author of some of the greatest religious poetry in the French language, also produced an erotic classic. The poetry of his *Erotic Works (Oeuvres Libres)*, sensual, outrageous, coarse, and tender, forms an integral part of his creative output. It is central to an understanding of his tragically divided nature.

The *Erotic Works* consists of three books. The first, *Les Amies*, a slender volume of six lesbian sonnets, was published in 1867 in Brussels. Twenty-three years later *Femmes* appeared, reflecting the mature poet's heterosexual encounters with Parisian female friends and prostitutes. *Hombres*, poems of male love written primarily in 1891, was published posthumously in 1903 (some sources give 1904).

The complete *Erotic Works* has long been unavailable to the general reader in one source, even though this collection (sometimes called *Trilogie érotique*) has circulated since 1910[1] in expensive, extremely rare editions often illustrated by well-known artists. Except for a few individual poems, Verlaine's erotic writings have been excluded from his so-called "Complete Works." The exceptions are the sonnets of *Les Amies*, as well as four poems from *Femmes* and two from *Hombres*, all of which were included in the collection of his poetry entitled *Parallèlement* (1889).

How can we possibly reconcile Verlaine's sordid personal life with his sublime books of verse—with the exquisite laments of *Poèmes saturniens*, the fairy-tale magic of *Fêtes galantes*, the spiritual depth of *Sagesse*, the poignant yearning of *Romances sans paroles*? Rampant, coarse sensuality, physical attacks on his wife, his mother, and his son, the shooting of his lover Arthur Rimbaud, a mania for drink—these were key themes of a life riddled with court trials, domestic strife, self-imposed poverty, vagabondage, chronic invalidism.

Verlaine's unashamedly erotic poems are a key to his strangely dual character. They are a forceful reminder that Verlaine was, as he called himself, a *homo-duplex*, a merging of opposites, a man torn between conventional morality and the quest for freedom, between heterosexuality and homosexuality, between religion and sex, between Baudelaire's "two postulates" of Satan and God.[2]

Verlaine's "rich, contradictory, tortured soul"[3] made him both saint and sinner. Once, immediately after attending a midnight mass, he went to a nearby café where he wrote a letter full of erotic and scatological jests which he decked out with drawings reminiscent of graffiti in a street urinal. Perhaps no poet ever used the words "chaste" and "chastity" more than Verlaine.[4] Yet, during periods when he was producing poems of worship, he also turned out erotic verses in which religious symbolism served blasphemous ends. We find religious symbols, for example, in "Through the Friendly Silence" (*Amies*), "Overture" and "To One Who Is Called Frigid" (*Femmes*), and in "Song of the Prick with Foreskin Pulled Back, I" and "A Bit of Shit" (*Hombres VIII*).

The favorite sin of the Absinthe-Tinted Poet was *gourmandise* or gluttony, sexual and otherwise. As a precocious fourteen-year-old he read obscene books and may have scribbled filthy verses. By age seventeen he was frequenting brothels. At eighteen he acquired the addiction to liquor which led to homicidal rages and blighted the rest of his life. Wild flings of debauchery would alternate with periods of remorse and atonement. In his last years, living in seedy Parisian boardinghouses and hospitals, it was not so unusual for Verlaine to go to bed on twenty successive days with twenty different women picked up at random.

Verlaine's dual nature was mirrored in his bisexuality. His bisexual orientation triggered the deepseated sense of guilt instilled by his proper bourgeois parents—his father an exemplary army officer, rather distant emotionally, and his possessive, overprotective mother who spoiled him.

The poet's homoerotic activity began in his teens and continued side by side with his heterosexual exploits until his marriage in 1870 to his devoted, conventional "child wife" Mathilde Mauté. During his brief period of settled domesticity, the "closet queen" fretted over his passing affairs with boys and mourned a slain ex-schoolmate whom he had dropped to marry Mathilde. After his tempestuous affair with Rimbaud, Verlaine continued to have numerous male lovers, a few emotionally close, most casual. The rural lovers of "Mille e Tre" may have been inspired by a period of freewheeling sexuality following his stint at farming with Lucien Létinois. This peasant youth whom Verlaine had considered adopting died of typhoid fever in 1883.

In *Les Amies,* Verlaine veiled his own homoerotic impulses behind descriptions of lesbian love. He wanted this little volume of verse to shock the conventionally minded, and it did cause a storm. To avoid the Second Empire's censors, the book was printed in Belgium, in December 1867, by Poulet-Malassis, publisher of Baudelaire and of anti-imperialist propaganda. Verlaine had signed himself pseudonymously as "the licentious Don Pablo Maria de Herlañes." Despite these precautions, the book was intercepted by the French customs on the way to Paris in May 1868; a Lille court condemned it as indecent literature and the whole shipment was destroyed.

To the modern reader, the tender, playful Girlfriends of *Amies* radiate a lascivious charm but can hardly be considered obscene. For these sonnets, Verlaine borrowed the vocabulary of Baudelaire, especially his "Femmes damnées" of *Les Fleurs du mal.* The influence of the Parnassian school of poets, who favored hard, objective verses about bygone times, is also evident, particularly in "Sappho." Even so, in his candid portrayal of supple, young, passionate bodies bathed in a delicate atmosphere, Verlaine was striking out into new territory.

Verlaine's sexual ambivalence is most noticeable in *Femmes.* In "To One Who Is Called Frigid" the poet drools over "the pretty, childlike nipples of a miss who's barely into puberty." His bedmate in "Whores I" excites him with her "masculine airs" and "farcically boyish ways." Rita in "For Rita" sports a mannish waist and small, hard breasts that seem to pose the question, "Homme ou femme?" One psychoanalytic critic has argued that Verlaine's passion for young girls is a disguised form of homosexuality.[5] Whatever truth there may be in this, only one poem of *Femmes*, "Perfumed Dish" ("Vas unguentatum"), is an expression of undiluted ecstasy.

Most of the pieces in *Femmes* are believed to have been written in the late 1880s. Around this time, Verlaine's affections and money were divided equally between two stocky, parasitical, middle-aged streetwalkers, Philomène Boudin (nicknamed Esther) and Eugénie Krantz (Mouton), both of whom may have inspired parts of *Femmes*.

In 1871 Verlaine received a letter, with several extraordinary poems enclosed, from a youth in Charleville named Arthur Rimbaud. "Come, dear, great soul, we are calling to you, we await you," Verlaine replied, enclosing a money order for Rimbaud's carfare to Paris. Into his life like a thunderbolt came the conceited, slovenly, deliberately crude sixteen-year-old brat with adorable blue eyes. Rimbaud, "ange et démon," was the dominant partner in the relationship, intellectually and physically. By some accounts, he performed such "tigeresque" acts as slashing Verlaine across the chest with a knife during sexual intercourse.

In their flight from bourgeois respectability, the visionary Rimbaud and his disciple wandered like tramps through France, Belgium, and England, provoking scorn and scandal. Their stormy, drunken affair, which wrecked Verlaine's marriage, ended for all practical purposes in 1873 when Verlaine was sentenced to two years in prison for wounding Rimbaud in the wrist with a revolver during an argument.

During his eighteen months' imprisonment, Verlaine, seeking deliverance from guilt, became an ardent convert to Catholicism. He hung a huge crucifix in his cell. This conversion was short-lived and his rampant physical appetites resurfaced, making a chaos of the last two decades of his life. This was the period during which he wrote *Femmes* and *Hombres*. These years were also his most prolific. Verlaine's public disgrace had marked the beginning of his full devotion to his muse.

The tongue-in-cheek "Sonnet to the Asshole" (*Hombres XV*), a collaborative effort of Verlaine and Rimbaud, dates from 1871. It was created for the *Album Zutique,* begun that year by the physician Antoine Cros, who invited a group of poets to meet together and recite their facetious verses, often parodies of each other's work. An eight-line version of "Innocent Verses" ("Dizain Ingénu") entitled "Remembrances" was also written in 1871 for the *Album Zutique.* "In This Café" (*Hombres XII*), although dated 1891, harks back to the two bohemian lovers jerking off in public in symbolic defiance of a society that condemned homosexuality. "To A Statue" was written in 1889, and "Rendez-vous," in an early version, in 1887. Verlaine probably wrote most of the rest of *Hombres* in 1891 during one of his sojourns at the Hôpital Broussais.

The poet's dual nature is reflected in his prolific output. *Parallèlement* (1889), a celebration of the demands and follies of sensual desire, was written as a complement to *Amour* (1888) and *Bonheur* (1891), works which sang of divine love. The title *Parallèlement*, besides denoting the physical running alongside the spiritual, also stood for the influence of Rimbaud moving parallel to that of Mathilde.[6] Similarly, the heterosexual *Femmes* and gay *Hombres* embody the theme of sexual parallelism. The last poem of *Femmes*, "Lesson (Abridged)," introduces the first of *Hombres*, "No Sacrilege, Poet," indicating that the second volume was meant to complement the first.

Verlaine's *Erotic Works*, though sexually explicit and sometimes intentionally gross, transcends pornography and achieves the status of literature. The collection has its flaws—the sonnets of *Amies* are slightly cloying, *Femmes* and *Hombres* are at times sophomoric, and a certain repetitiousness (the fatal weakness of pornography) creeps in. Nevertheless, in these poems Verlaine creates a strange, compulsive beauty by embracing sexuality (and bisexuality) with a hearty candor that is all the more exceptional coming at a time when the morbid and the effete were deliberately cultivated.[7]

Verlaine was a founder of the Symbolist movement, a true Decadent before the full flowering of turn-of-the-century Decadence. The Prince of Poets (as Verlaine was called after the death of Leconte de Lisle) was the last great bohemian. He threw himself lustily into women, men, religion, intoxication, and poetry with equal passion. A child of the Romantic period, he helped define the modern age, and his explicitly erotic poetry is remarkable for the modern note it strikes, born of the tension between unlimited personal freedom and guilt.

In contrast to *Femmes* and *Hombres*, Verlaine's tamer, nonexplicit erotic books of the 1890s are mostly poor to mediocre. However, one noteworthy feature these works share, to varying degrees, with *Femmes* and *Hombres* is the curious mixture of street slang, foreign words, archaisms, and argot in which Verlaine took obvious delight. With this potent word brew, he dissolved the stuffy traditions of Romantic rhetoric inspired by Victor Hugo, just as he mocked (in the savagely witty *Hombres XIV*) the sexualization of language.

In this translation, an attempt was made to bring over in a contemporary idiom Verlaine's mixture of coarseness and elegance, his esoteric sexual slang, puns, and wordplay, while remaining as close as possible to the literal meaning of the originals. The French text for this volume is based principally on *Oeuvres Libres: Première édition critique*[8] and *Oeuvres poétiques complètes.*[9] In some instances, what was deemed the best variant was used after comparison of available texts of *Oeuvres Libres.*

Alan Stone

Paul Verlaine

Friends

ON THE BALCONY

The twosome watched the swallows take wing;
one raven-haired with skin like milk,
one all blonde and rosy, their silk
nightgowns loosely undulating.

While asphodels lay languishing
and the soft, round moon climbed uphill,
both savored the sad bliss of guiltless
hearts and the stillness of the evening.

Moist arms girdling each other's waist,
odd couple pitying those more chaste,
thus on the balcony the young girls dreamt.

Behind them, in the dark, opulent room,
matching an empress's throne for pomp,
the perfumed Bed lay waiting in the gloom.

AT BOARDING SCHOOL

A September evening, sultry, warm;
one was sixteen, the other one year less,
slim, strawberry-cheeked, blue-eyed misses
who slept together in the student dorm.

For comfort's sake, each had torn off
her amber-scented shift. The younger lass
stoops, arms stretched; her tutoress
kisses her while cupping breasts grown warm

then falls upon her knees, goes wild,
and, mouth glued to the womb of that child,
darts her tongue in the dusky, blond-gold bush.

On dainty fingers the novice, meanwhile,
ticks off promised waltzes till, blushing,
she flashes an innocent little smile.

THROUGH THE FRIENDLY SILENCE

Long white muslin curtains that flit,
there in the night lamp's pale light,
like an opalescent wave adrift
on the eerie shadows of the night.

The curtains of Adeline's vast bed shift,
Claire, to your silver tones so bright,
your caressing voice interlaced with
a voice scaling wild, frenzied heights.

"Love, let's love!" your mingled murmurs chime,
Claire, Adeline, darling victims of
the noble vow made by your souls sublime.

Love, then, dear recluses, love
since even you, in these dismal times, feel
the holy Stigmata mark you with their weal.

SPRING

The randy, russet-haired miss,
turning to the blonde who seems
the image of her pristine dreams,
softly, achingly whispers this:

"Your puberty's a bower of bliss
where bright buds toss and white sap streams.
Let my fingers go roving midst
the moss where your fair rosebud gleams.

"Lost in slender grass, let me,
darling, lap the dewdrops which
lave your flower in its niche

"till I see bright ecstasy
steal across those features shy
like dawn upon the morning sky."

SUMMER

And the girl, tenderly caressed
by her panting mistress, swoons,
and her skin all atremble, moans:
"I'm dying, O my mistress!

"I'm dying from your hot, firm breasts
which leave me drunk and powerless,
and from your lusty flesh whereon
breathes a rich and rare cologne.

"Your body has the dark allure
of summer fruit grown luscious, full,
amber, somber, ripe, mature.

"Your voice booms mid sultry squalls
and the blood-red of your auburn hair
abruptly flees on the slow night air."

10

SAPPHO

Frenzied, breasts taut, eyes grown sore,
Sappho, vexed by the languor of her passion,
runs like a she-wolf along the freezing shore.

She dreams of Phaon, blind to her normal fashion
of love, and, brooding on each slighted tear,
pulls out by the fistful her wildly flowing hair.

In angry self-reproach she ceaselessly weeps
for the days when her love's chaste glory
was celebrated far and wide in poetry
whispered by the soul to virgins fast asleep.

Then, wan eyelids lowered, she leaps
into the waters where Fate calls, while pale Selene
bursts forth above and ignites the dark sea,
avenging all lovers who sapphic trysts keep.

Women

14

OVERTURE

O whores, true priestesses of the One Deity,
I'd like to be tucked inside your asses and thighs,
be ye novices or pros, plain or fancy,
in your cracks and crannies I'd live out my days
     and nights.

Your marvelous feet, hot on the trail for a client,
rest only when you're stretched out with a lover,
afterwards you rub them against his feet, pliant,
as, breathless and weary, he nestles under the covers.

Feet kissed, inhaled, fondled, licked from
the ankles and the lakes of sluggish veins
to the soles, to toes sucked one by one,
feet more shapely than a heroine's or saint's!

I worship, for their charming pranks, your mouths
with tongues and lips and agile teeth that skim
our tongues or maybe even go down south
for pastimes almost as sweet as shoving it in.

And your breasts, twin peaks of lust and pride between
which my virile pride sometimes swells
to graze there at ease or poke its head
like a wild boar roaming Parnassus' and Pindus' dells.

15

Your arms, I worship, too, those lovely snow-white
  arms,
firm, plump, sinewy, with a dainty bloom
whose whiteness like your asses wholly disarms,
hot when we screw, afterwards cool as a tomb.

And the hands that come with your arms, these I
  adore!
Hands blessed to be both lazy and lewd,
breathing new life into cocks gone cold and sore,
masturbators of infinite solicitude!

Yet whores, Holy of Holies, tabernacles of sex,
all this pales before your asses and cunts
whose odor and feel and taste and loveliness
exalt your disciples to the rank of Chosen Ones.

And that's why, sisters, in your asses and thighs
I bid you to tuck me in, my good old lays;
be ye plain or fancy, novices or pros,
in your cracks and crannies I'd live out my nights and
  days.

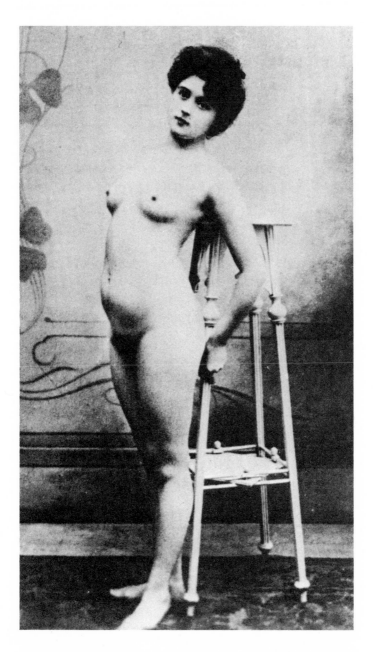

17

TO ONE WHO IS CALLED FRIGID

You're not the juiciest of all
who've sucked my lollipop,
you're not the most delectable
of this last winter's crop,

but all the same I worship you!
Your soft, kind body's sovereign
composure brings to view
all that's freely feminine

and sensuous for nights on end,
from your feet tenderly kissed
to those clear eyes that portend
no orgasms but much bliss!

From your legs and thighs pleasing
with their unripened flesh
full of odors of wet cheese
and crayfish, fine and fresh

(dainty, modest Little Thing
tinted lightly by a golden frill
in divine splendor opening
to my brutal, dumb will)

up to the darling tits of a miss
who's scarcely into puberty,
to your slim Venus bust which
ravishes triumphantly,

past gleaming shoulders to your mouth
to your childish mug which cracks
innocent simpers not borne out
by your far from innocent acts,

to your fine, tangled curls
like the locks of a handsome boy
falling loose in careless twirls
that carry a promise of joy,

down a lazy spine plump
for fondling to the sheer abyss
of sacred whiteness, glorious rump
whose soft curves recall your chisel,

O Canova! back to those thighs
it's only proper to praise again,
to your calves, firm delights,
to your toenails pink and golden!

Were our couplings indissoluble?
No, but they had a certain charm.
Were the fires we lit unquenchable?
No, but at least they kept us warm.

And your clit, cold? Rather, cool.
No wonder our hottest fornication
(dreaming of which makes me drool)
was only a better masturbation

though my thousand little kindnesses
got you moist and ready with no
undue acts of naughtiness,
sexy schoolgirl who thrilled me so.

I count you dear among my women,
hope tempering my regret
till the day when we'll love again
and get each other good and wet.

FOURSOME

From the small of the back to the fall of chaste, puerile
    dreams:
  Ass, fond throne of lechery;
Ass, your curves ennobled by their white purity,
Prouder than any face your two cheeks gleam!

Breasts, twin mountains of milk and azure whose
    tawny peaks
  overlook the valley and the sacred grove!
Breasts with sweet tips dangling apples of love
savored by lips and tongues grown drunk on the
    feast!

Ass cleft by a smart crevice oozing pink shade
  where desire, gone mad, now lurks about;
beloved pillows whose deep fold comforts snouts
or tools, cool oasis for hands after countless escapades!

Breasts, fine banquets for hands crammed with
    goodies,
  huge, heavy breasts, a bit mocking in their
    complacency,
poised, swaying, swollen with pride of victory,
flashing coy tits over our kneeling bodies!

Ass, your buttocks truly the breasts' big sisters,
     though more at ease,
   more good-natured, full of smiles,
not too mischievous or prone to the wiles
of power, since your beauty casts its own harsh
     tyrannies!

Well now, sweet despots, all you four, en masse,
   queenly, regal, to whom the rabble bend the knee
while you anoint your worshipful devotees,
Praise and glory to you, O holy breasts, O majestic ass!

TRIOLET TO A VIRTUOUS WOMAN . . .

By the bulkiness of my affection
don't measure my manly skill;
I'm sure my size is no reflection
of the bulkiness of my affection.
Kindly squeeze my erection
'twixt your fur and your frill.
By the bulkiness of my affection
don't measure my manly skill.

Quality counts more, they say,
than quantity, however whopping.
Fie on gluttons, praise the gourmet!
Quality counts more, they say,
so just cooperate and may
your wildest fancies keep us hopping.
Quality counts more, they say,
than quantity, however whopping.

A little fish swells in size
so long as One gives it vim.
Be that One, and for your prize
a little fish swells in size.
To bait of quim watch porgy rise
like a proud, athletic limb.
A little fish swells in size
so long as One gives it vim.

My prick mocks your silly pride,
being proud and full of pluck.
You can mourn its size inside.
My prick mocks your silly pride
as it jeers a puss, one-eyed,
staving off an anal fuck.
My prick mocks your silly pride,
being proud and full of pluck.

Even so, in a wink, it's done!
Meadows are soaked. Calm prevails.
Saber drawn and roar of drums,
even so, in a wink, it's done!
Nonetheless despite our fun
your pride bleeds, my prick wails.
Even so, in a wink, it's done.
Meadows are soaked. Calm prevails.

26

ROYAL TASTES

Louis the Fifteenth didn't like perfumes much.
Like him I let my women dab on a mere touch.
No scent bottles, please, or sachets for romance!
But give me a body that exudes a sharp fragrance
naturally, provided it keeps my firmness fresh;
and with every exposure of the coveted flesh
my refined taste applauds as my lust feeds
on the odor of pubescence and brave deeds
or on the good musty smell of ripe women.
I even worship (Conscience, hush your clamor!)
how shall I say it . . . these secret aromas of vulva
and its environs, both before and after
the divine bear hug, and during the squeeze too,
however it feels, or seems, or ought to.
Then, when my sense of smell, by bliss ravished
    again,
dozes off like my other senses, and when
my eyes grow dim while gazing on one
whose eyes do likewise, memento and omen
of a lattice of arms and legs entwined neat,
pink feet cuddling under the damp sheets,
from this yet more sensuous languor rises
a human stench which, though scandalous, is
so terrific you'd think you were eating it raw!
What need, then, for some evil potion drawn,
sweet-scented, from some animal or plant
to make one's brain buzz and one's heart grow
    faint,
since, to amplify the thrill of ecstasy,
I've distilled the very quintessence of beauty!

WHORES I

Sweet, simple prostitute,
I'll take you over all those sluts

who fill up sidewalks I wouldn't use
to scrape the crud from off my shoes,

those dumb, pretentious rag dolls
who're just skirts with tawdry souls

full of horse races and bets,
a plague all of Paris gets!

You're my only real chum
and though the darkness softens you some

you keep a masculine air about you
even with bedsheets wrapped about you,

a mistress short on ceremonies,
a lover and a sometime tease

cajoling me as well you must
to fan my sagging carnal lust.

29

Your manners, like your motions, flirt,
are so grotesquely boyish, pert,

that one might think our screwing a sin
(pardoned since it's neatly hidden)

except you've got that robust ass,
fresh round arms, hips that pass,

and make up for what you're missing
with plain old-fashioned hugs and kissing.

Good soul, good pal, in more than name,
so pure, so constant is your flame

you'd lend some hard-up prick a hand
with the meager funds at your command

even if it meant doubling your lays
or pawning off your negligees!

Like us you've had your share of woe;
your tears, our moans, together flow;

our tears, melting in your moans,
chime obscene and tender tones,

and the sympathy you spend on us
makes you truly virtuous.

A brother to me, a lady too,
and as my wife you now will do . . .

Well, puss, till dawn, let's not stir,
let's curl up into a ball and purr!

Lie close to feel my extra limb
snug against your ass's rim,

our knees tightly intertwined,
your childish feet limp between mine.

Roll your ass under your gown,
leaving the hand I've shoved way down

in the warmth of your fine underbrush.
There! We're silent, in a hush.

A truce, no peace, reigns supreme.
You're sleeping? Quite. No bad dreams

while I doze off, trembling with bliss,
my nose nestled against your frizz.

WHORES II

And you, you'll do nicely too,
despite your manners, rough, crude,
which aren't the mark of a prude
but of a domineering shrew.

Yes, you'll do although
your mannish voice rattles off
the highs and lows of a drunkard's cough,
you drunk with arms akimbo!

But woman! Holy shit! You turn
our heads around, fucking us
whenever you feel adventurous.
Shit! Our blood does burn!

Beneath black rep you proudly boast
(unless, of course, it's foam rubber)
those big bazooms, pliant, chubby,
hard, tempting, they're the most!

Your belly, sagging to nyloned thighs,
ends in two fine meat-pâtés
which earn from me a gourmet's praise
like fish decked in sauce and spice.

33

Your white stockings (and you deserve
applause for shunning the gaudy kind)
nearly make us go stark blind
from gaping at those bulging curves!

Your brunette's face whose weary features
are a certain indication
you prefer your copulations
with the brawniest of creatures—

Your glances, slyly innocent,
which moisten our eyes, next our cocks
until besotted bastards flock
to you, pure and reverent—

Your whole form—from arched soles
bent upward to our embraces,
to dyed bangs to pockmarked face
which our kisses drill with holes—

makes old geezers' pants get wet
and hardens up the hot young men
we once were and are again,
jerking us like marionettes

and making us full-fledged scholars who
crowd around your ass to stoop
and gobble up your flesh like soup,
ready to croak beneath your shoe!

You get us flustered pretty quick
but since we're slower on the uptake
you warm us with your wiles to bake
ragouts full of cunt and prick.

Though cruel at heart, you do bestow
indulgences by the bedful!
With lowlife you're duly dreadful,
you make things really start to flow.

Vampire, you suck us (or so you say)
not to please yourself, but more
so that we suckers know the score
about the nicest ways to lay.

We do the duties we're assigned
cause in the end you fuck us out
if only to turn aside our snouts
for a younger bunch of swine.

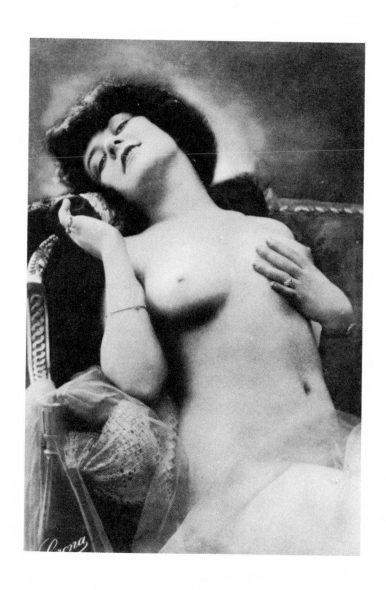

TO MADAME ———

When you engulf my head or thighs
in your thighs, or numb
my throat with the rare delights
of your fresh, astringent come,

or bite my not too big cock,
a bruiser from balls to tip,
with your cunt which tightly locks
my master key in its grip,

you wriggle your ass in a way
no married dame could imitate
amid our cunt and cock tongue-play
(hell, your wiggle sets me straight!)

Your copulatory tongue
explores my mouth so slowly
and with such volcanic hunger
Shit! it blisters my soul.

And your cunt grabs my cock
like a bear would suck a titty,
a well-licked bear whose fleecy mop
is a rug where mine sits pretty.

A well-licked bear, greedy, drunk,
this my roving tongue will swear,
since your beady clit's upsprung,
worried more than it could bear.

Well-licked, sure, but rough and surly
those shapely, teasing pussy-lips
smiling red mid black so curly
like a harlequin's cherry lips.

PERFUMED DISH

Gaze fondly on the moiré cleft
whose pale rosy tints suffice
to mark out my trajectory
into Mohammed's Paradise.

O my weary eyes, impatient
with humdrum vistas, and sullen quite,
imbibe, with an artist's delectation,
this opulent, enchanted sight:

a jewel box trimmed with black plush
curving like a pleated hem,
spangled with a copper blush,
a jewel, god of all gems,

throbbing with vigor and white sap,
wafting a perfume that has to be
right out of Mother Nature's lap
to drive the lover to ecstasy.

Stare awhile, then breathe in deep,
now comes the time for more love,
bright bud ever bursting its sheath,
smiling ruby, flower of

conscience, baby brother of one
that's hotly kissed and squeezed,
the two going at their fun
till both of them can only wheeze . . .

But take a rest cause you're on fire.
Likewise how to lull the friend
that breasts, legs, womb, thighs
stew and simmer without end?

Dear me, its playmate's drunken bliss
gets me up and going when
my meat rises from one kiss . . .
Come on, we'd better start again!

FASHIONABLE DALLIANCE

With eager hands
the roguish chit
jerks off her urchin
chum a bit.

The happy schoolboy,
head all bare,
comes and sputters
everywhere.

The beaming lass,
thrilled to see
this milk but wondering
what it might be,

sucks a drop
from the very tip.
Hold on! No shit!
Zounds! Let 'er rip!

She slurps and kisses
the pretty stump
then done with this
she rams the pump!

Little viscount
of love's-so-grand
don't boast about
this one-night-stand,

fine flower of
romantic sprees
midsummer recess
in the 90's:

Such escapades
in starry castles
your schoolfellows,
even the asses,

could freely summon
up for you
by the score, and every
word of it true;

and your girl cousins,
fallen angels,
the poor sweethearts
are no strangers

to wafers sucked
and juices spent
since first communion
came and went:

but try to make them
commit the sin—
pricks, they make you
hold it in.

44

POPULAR TABLEAU

The homely, scrawny-looking apprentice boy, just
      fifteen,
winsome in his rough, listless ways, eyes keen
and deep-set, complexion dull, yanks from his britches
his already hugely swollen cock which itches
and mounts the fat, still pretty proprietress
as she swoons on the bed in indecent undress,
legs high, breasts bare, she gives him a sign!
Judging by the way the kid's ass grinds
and the even, treading motion of his dangling feet
it's plain to see he's not afraid to ram it deep
or to knock up this dame who couldn't give a fuck
(her cuckold husband's making big bucks).
Reaching the crowning height of ecstasy
she squeals with rapture, "You've made me
a baby, I feel it, and I love you all
the more for it!" "Now let me try your baptismal
sweets!" she begs afterwards, then gladly sprawls
on her ass to press and cuddle and kiss his balls.

LOVE NOTE FOR LILY

My good little townswoman,
tonight I was hoping you'd visit me,
do knock on my door and come in
and we'll go on a shameful spree
of quick or leisurely lays just
geared to satisfy my lusts,
likewise your daintier itch.
First I'll kiss your lips (guess which?)
polishing off my whole dessert,
and I'll be sure to exert
myself like I always do
with a bold technique that's subtle too!
You'll run your pretty fingers
through my reddish-brown apostle's beard
while I stroke and play with yours,
and on your lily-white breast where
my passion makes roses sprout
I'll plant my incandescent mouth.
My arms, summoning their skill,
will dizzily hug the goodies
below your waist and lower still.
Then my hands, after sparring
with hands hot for battle,
will dole out a fond spanking
to your gorgeous ass which, full
to bursting, will pull
my gravity-beam to your center.
My turn to knock. O whisper: "Enter!"

FOR RITA

I detest skinny women
but Rita, you're terrific!
O girl whose somewhat Negroid lips
shows your lust's prolific.

Your black hair's so obscene
because it's so very pretty
and your eyes mirror shifting scenes
smacking (heavens!) of heresy.

These eyes, dark yet gleaming
through frolics shamefully lewd,
sparkle with cuntish laughter
and with perfect charm exude

looks clueing super studs in
to techniques none dare mention:
"Whatever you may dare, follow
your ass's every last intention."

Above your masculine waist
that's just a bit too slight
hang your boobs, confused Sodom
beckoning then drawing tight.

In a sinfully tight blouse
your small hard breasts of a statue
raise the question, "Man or woman?"
to the studs gaping at you.

Yet your legs are quite feminine,
plumping up as they curve higher
to gracefully merge into your ass,
tame plaything of my desire

tucked in the sexy folds of a skirt
ruffled by whorish design
to bare more than it covers
a smooth belly to cushion mine!

In sum, your whole being oozes
hungers, flames, thirsts alone.
But I'm randier: what say
you weigh your charms against my own?

Hurry then, to bed, my princess.
There! Let's wage ecstatic war
till morning comes, and then decide
which of us is the bigger whore.

AT THE BALL

A dream of women's thighs
having for ceiling and sky
the asses and cunts of lovely
dames who go traipsing by

in a gaudy swirl of skirts
to ballads bawdy enough,
and the asses have such cracks
and the cunts such furry muffs!

White stockings on firm calves
so pleasing and cockteasing,
and, higher up, those huge,
dangling baubles ripe for seizing,

and arching ankle boots
(big feet tucked snug inside)
leading the stately dance
with a quick if weary slide.

A most peculiar odor,
sweet and foul at once—
essence of come, asshole,
sweat from toes and cunts,

and skin perfume—
floats on the sultry air,
making us fucking mad
like Jews whose heads are bare.

See how cosy I am
stretched out completely flat.
At this delightful ball
my body is a mat

for ball-breaking dancers
who as a dumb
joke twirl over me
when my turn comes.

What a treat for both
them and me! Mangled?
Far from it, it's a
pleasant, mild tingle

of half a million strokes
of tiny feet prancing
over your legs, balls,
stomach, and your thing!

The songs die, the dancing
stops. Now big shitters
flaunt their ample charms
and God! One of them sits

right on my face!
My tongue roves between two
divine ports of entry
to gobble succulent stews.

Asses row upon row,
each in its own way,
upon me freely bestow
this real feast for a real gourmet.

I wake up, touch myself . . .
my pulse runs at a trot.
Goddamn make-believe lay!
Goddamn smelly twat!

53

54

SURRENDER

I'm fucked out. You've captured my soul.
Now I love only your fat asshole
sniffed, licked, and poked a whole lot,
and your dear cunt stoked by my hot
hand or cock—cause I'm not the sort
who goes in for Sodom/Gomorrah sport,
I'm more into Paphos/Lesbos play
(Your pussy's almost been licked away).
What hooked me were your gorgeous boobs,
heavy bazooms my hands cup
for my thirsty lips to lap up
the way a guy takes a swig of ale.
I suck those tits, first hard, then limp,
a change of pressure like the crimp that can get into
    lengthy cocks.
Hot pricks need some real knocks
whether woman-on-top, at top
speed, doggie-fashion like a pet,
or in the style of Marie Antoinette,
so let's invent new positions till
morning comes, beloved despot
whose every desire is heavenly respite,
hellish delight that brings my death

besides knocking me out of breath
and all to appease your hungry twat.
Come pours from Old Blind Bob
like blood from a wound. So what!
As long as my soul throbs
and my heart beats (while blood runs faster)
I want to be your slave in all I do,
having, cruel mistress, in you
a mistress no more, but a master.

DAINTY FEASTS

Cross your thighs over my face
in such a way that my tongue,
silencing its silly prattle,
can't do anything but feast
on come-juice and taste of dung
which have made me forever yours
as I'm ravished by your whole
body, by your carnal soul,
and by your meat-eating mind which
devours all that's best in me,
making me more of a bitch
than any lily-white whore,
as pure now as in those days
years back before our first lays.
There, primp up and show
by some contented gesture
that deep down you love your old
dog or at least put up with
his pussy-licking (clit too)
and anus-chew, just like
some younger stud might do
who's better hung but less of a pro
in fucking theory and practice.
O your cunt! It smells so good!
Digging in with nose and muzzle
I romp around and take deep whiffs
and splutter and drool and poke and nuzzle
and sniff and slobber and O! I guzzle
in your pig-scented cunt

topped by your auburn mount
and fleeced with fine reddish down
leading to the marvelous hole
where I splutter and drool and poke and nuzzle
and sniff and slobber and even guzzle
with the painstaking devotion
and hot zeal of a slave freed
from every prick-restricting creed.
The charming furrow that I've licked
amoroso from the loins
down to the deep well
where I tarry a long spell
to make the usual devotions
carries me straight to the joyful
slash of my whorish lass.
There, in a positively
exotic tongue, I salaam
your oozing clit in an accent
so fine that my nether-head,
provoked by this oral intercourse,
spouts forth creamy rhetoric
but rests its case upon this premise.
And then I doze between your thighs
which you've spread, weary, relaxed
through all our tender loving acts.

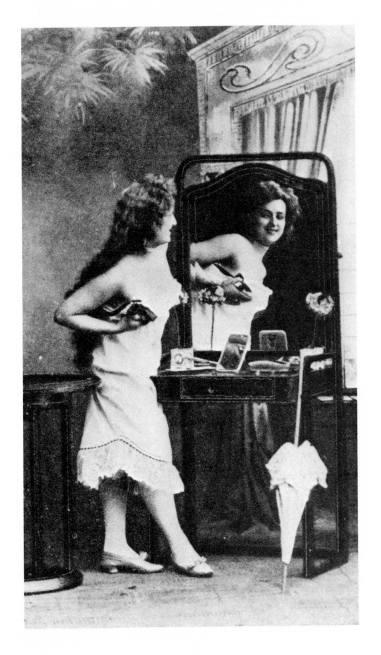

GAMES WITH YOU ON TOP

Since it's comfier to fuck
with you on top, I really go
for it, even more so
when I use my little trick

of getting a grip on your fat ass
and tickling your big ripe
cheeks a little so as
to smooth my way down your path.

Next my shaft gets plumb drunk
from your cunt's wet kisses
and your corpulent belly
sloshing around in the gunk.

Drunk, too, on tits bursting
out of your shift to bob
slowly up and down before
my eyes so huge they're fairly bursting,

while your eyes, like antique Juno's
orbs, cowlike and dumb,
prick mine with sidelong glances
that cut as deep as hatchet blows

until I'm wholly mesmerized
and my partner down south
after a bit of hand-in-mouth
is completely petrified.

And then I shudder and come inside
this living nightmare of meat,
a dainty yet slobbering treat
by turns narrow and wide,

flesh rising and sinking to press
its bouncy weight against my balls
so that my stumbling cock, seized
by a flash of hot dizziness

midst all this jism and come-juice
dies, revives, dies again;
revives, redies, revives again
from all this jism and come-juice!

Meanwhile my fingers, having
rapped upon your asshole
lightly as butterflies yet
O so tender and loving,

and my palms, cooling somewhat
from your ass, climb *lento*
back up toward your boobs
and stroke to get them both hot.

ADORATION

I'm laid out full-length on her smooth bed.
Daylight has come. My yearning to wed
this pretend-wife, my persevering
prick, hot ass, all seem bawdier, more
glaring in the mounting dawn that breaks
on our ever-expanding nocturnal feast.
She's squatting naked on my face for a good
licking, because last night I was a good
boy, and this—cunt's an aphrodisiac!—
is her royal way of paying me back.
I said royal, but I meant divine:
Buttocks, ripe pulp, skin, flesh sublime,
potently pure globes, white, rich, blue-streaked,
furrow with cock-lifting smell, dim pink,
lazy, broad, a fine place to nest, I should think!
Last feast, dessert of cunt meringue whipped higher
by my frenzied tongue strumming the folds like a lyre!
These buttocks again, like two half moons
mysterious, joyful, where from now on
I'd like to build a nest for my poet's dreams,
my horny heart, and my fancy schemes
while my mistress, or better yet, master, sits
    enthroned
on me, her rapt trainbearer, completely owned.

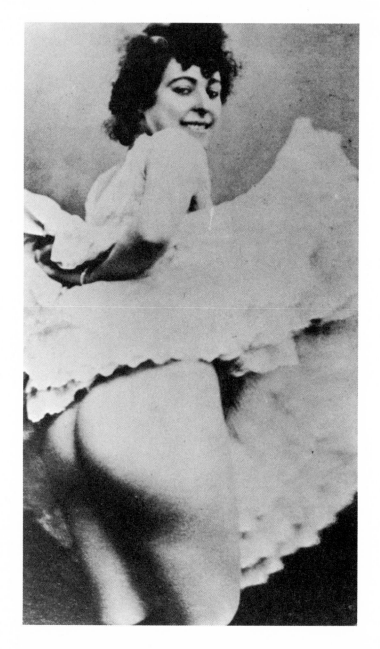

LESSON (ABRIDGED)

A pretty blonde head reeling with bliss
on a gurgling neck above sexy tits,
dark medallions of breasts hot to be kissed,
this torso propped against pillows while betwixt
two legs pointing skyward, quivering mass,
a woman on her knees—rapt in foreplay
only Love can teach—to the gods displays
the pure, unvarnished epic of her gorgeous ass,
mirror of beauty spotless and divine.
Female ass, serene victor of the male rump
whether it's a young boy's or teenager's hump,
female ass, ass of all asses, O holy shrine!

Men

I

No sacrilege, poet, keep this in mind:
Women are pretty, of course, and well worth the effort.
Even the fat ones' asses do them credit,
asses I, for one, have savored many a time.

What a love nest are these rumps (tits too!).
On my knees I hug one, lick the anus clean
while my fingers rummage in that other ravine.
And O how lewd these languidly gorgeous boobs!

Then too, an ass, especially in bed, serves well
as auxiliary to the knobs, the hairy patch,
and the box equipped with its spiral spring to snatch
a man and pull him deeper inside his chosen belle.

My hands, arms, legs, feet relax, aglow,
next to cheeks of such curvy, fresh spring
as befits the sexy altar where prowling
desire, obeying racy vows, skips to and fro.

But just compare this sweet ass, more expedient
than voluptuous—compare this big rear
to that flower of joy and beauty, the male derrière.
Flaunt this male ass most to the crushed and obedient!

"It's shameful!" Love objects. The Voice of History
replies: Male Ass, chaste pride of Hellas,
divine emblem of the true Rome, holier
still to dead Sodom, martyr to its glory.

After Shakespeare thrust aside Desdemona,
Cordelia, and Ophelia, his virile soul
celebrated in regal verse—let fools scold—
the masculine torso, and sang it glad hosannas.

The Valois were hot for men, and in our own day
Europe, although grown so bourgeois
and womanish, worshiped Ludwig of Bavaria,
the virgin king whose great heart beat ever so gay.

The Flesh (even woman's body) proclaims
the young virgin's ass, gaze, cock, form so bold,
and that, poet, is why, as Rousseau was told,
you ought to take a breather from those horny dames.

MILLE E TRE

My lovers aren't members of the gentry,
they're common laborers from suburbs or farms,
fifteen to twentyish, no frills, but with plenty
of brute vigor and rough, cocky charms.

Virile in dungarees and coats—their work clothes—
it's not perfume but health they ooze, pure and simple;
their gait, though rather lumbering, goes
in a poised, springy fashion, young and nimble.

With friendly mischief their cunning eyes twinkle
while their wet lips, full of robust kisses,
mouth slyly naive sweet nothings sprinkled
for good measure with a few "shits" and "pisses."

Their long strong guns and nice hot buns
delight my dork and asshole every night.
By dawnlight or lamplight their gleeful·guns
set my sagging, unconquered passions aright.

Thighs, souls, hands, my topsy-turvy brain,
feet, hearts, backs, ears, noses, traces
of nights, guts—all howl a refrain
and tread a wild jig in those boys' mad embraces.

Wild jig, mad refrain, more heaven's gift
than hell's, more infernal than sublime
—dizzied by this dancing I drift
in their rivulets of sweat, on their breath I climb.

My two Charleses—one a frisky tiger, eyes of a cat,
altar boy of sorts turning into an old blade;
the other a fine fellow, an impudent brat,
you only get randy when I go for your blade.

Odilon, street kid who's hung like a man,
your feet worship mine which burn even more
for your toes, still more for your can,
good and husky, but O those perfect feet I adore!

Fine, caressing phalanxes, satin-smooth
beneath the soles, around the ankles, branching where
arches flow with veins, and those strange, soothing
kisses of four feet having one soul, I swear!

Anthony, legendary in phallic size,
my triumphant king, god whom I revere
piercing my heart with your big blue eyes,
piercing my ass with your iron-tipped hunting spear.

Paul, blond athlete, pectorals resplendent
on a creamy chest whose hard tits I suck
same as your spout; Francis, sheaves of wheat bending
are your dancer's legs as shapely as your cock!

Augustus (a killer when we were just scratching
our first pubes) grows manlier with each new day;
Jules, your pale beauty makes you a bit bitchy;
Henry, stunning recruit who's off, drats! to the fray.

And all you lovers, whether had in a throng,
one by one, or alone—clear vision of the past,
present lusts, future stretching long,
no end to you sweethearts, yet never enough ass!

SONG OF THE PRICK . . .

I

It's just a smaller heart
with its tip in the air,
symbol proud and fair,
tender aching heart.

Its teardrops so large
sear like flames of hell,
longer than a farewell,
white as cunt discharge.

In a violet crown clad,
if only it would stay!
Such delight comes our way
when it wants to be had.

Like a priest with handsful
of oil at high mass
whose blessings now pass
from altar to chancel.

It wears its sacred ring,
amethyst and jism,
from night's dark chasm
to the dawn's awakening.

73

Then when mass is said,
discharged well and good,
it furls back its hood
on its pretty head.

II

Glans, high point of the soul
    of my lord,
of my beloved boy,
by you my happy asshole
    is bored
with a mixture of dread and joy.

(Anus drilled so long
    as some wrong
swells, straightens, and, full of pride
over brave, manly deeds
    parts cheeks
and savagely thrusts inside.)

Salter of red, meaty cunt,
    eternal font
my lips juicily lick,
glans, gross dainty
    no modesty
can spoil—now, you prick,

delicious glans, come, lift
    your shaft
of hot caressing mauve silk
rigged out by my hand
    in one grand
flourish with opal and milk.

It's just to milk my prick
    real quick
that I summon you today.
What's this! Your heat sizzles,
    I fizzle!
Goodbye to curds and whey!

Your whims none may foretell:
    Again you swell
mouth and anus wanting more;
now here they are, all set,
    in a sweat
for you, unvanquished lord.

Glans, nectar made to console
    my soul,
go back in your foreskin, slow
like a god into his cloud.
    I'm bowed
before you, reverent, as you go.

TO A STATUE

What's this! in this peaceful spa
—repose, quiet, calm, a truce indeed—
it's you, whether viewed from front or rear,
my handsome little pet: Ganymede!

The eagle transports you—reluctantly,
it seems—from your flowery knoll;
the even, thrifty motion of its wings
suggests that your ultimate goal

is not that despot Jove's lofty realm
but maybe Revard's lesser height.
The eagle's eyes, mocking passersby,
fix you queerly with their piercing sight.

Enough! Stay with us, dear boy.
Come now, help us to smother
our ennui with contagious joy,
for truly, aren't you our little brother?

RENDEZ-VOUS

In the still fateful room
of the house still breathing fate
where reason and virtue loom
far too long, far too late,

he seems to be awaiting some
familiar presence soon to be.
Glumly doubting it will come,
he murmurs quaveringly:

"Your voice trumpets in my soul
and your eyes set my heart aflame.
It's sinful, say all pure souls.
Master, I don't give a damn!

"Delight and sorrow, these are mine
and mine once more this mocking love,
a love full of sneers and whines,
my frisky, handsome wolf cub!

"Once you did come, wild youth,
as glib as you are graceful,
with cunning body and mouth
which violate me in all

"my concern for your extremely
tender age and your still
pubescent soul. You even
reamed my brute manly will.

"Two or three years have flown,
time enough to swell with sap
your virgin buds and to tone up
those lungs so prone to collapse.

"Every minute will be great,
for what a bruiser you will be!
If only you'd come! But traitor
you vow, you assure: 'Count on me.'

"You swear by heaven and earth to show,
then you miss our lover's tryst.
O this time, come! bow low
to my madly gyrating lusts.

"Into my fond arms steal,
Messiah, do come to me.
A rare and succulent meal
awaits you, come, you'll see!"

Phosphorus sets his eyes aglow
and his lips, with a grin perverse,
press the barbs of the quill he holds
while scrawling these lines of verse . . .

79

VII

Mount me like my little wife
who'd screw with me underneath.
There, that's it, are you all set
as my prick slides in, a knife

in butter, this way at least
I can kiss your lips and do
savage tongue-kissing,
smutty and yet so sweet!

Plunged inside your gaze my eyes
fathom the depths of your heart.
Lustful eyes return triumphant
from their lewd reveries.

I stroke your back, sinews bare,
flanks hot and cool, your nape,
the dainty curlicues under
your armpits, and your tousled hair!

The soft load of your shitshoot
straddles my thighs, melts into them
while my whang is frolicking
solely to make you hit the roof.

And you do get off, my pet,
for I espy your handsome tool
eager to get into the act,
quick, quick, it swells, grows fat,

stiffens, God! one drop, a pearly
forerunner, comes to glisten
at your glans's rosy tip. And I
must swallow it since mine's unfurling

in a foamy flux. Well, my fate
is rushing to grab between my lips
your cherished, fever-ridden dork
unloading itself in a royal spate.

Supreme milk, phosphor divine
whose fragrance of almond blossoms arouses
a harsh thirst that calls forth
this thirst for you consuming me blind.

The gift of your adolescence
passes, rich and bountiful, after
sanctifying with holy oil
my whole being drunk on your essence.

VIII

A bit of shit, a bit of cheese
aren't going to abash
my nose or mouth or make me cease
from joyfully tonguing cock or ass.

My lovers' assholes' smell is quite
a jolly treat, on the whole,
like tart, fresh apples overripe
whose healthy moisture makes them drool.

And my tongue, quick, untamed,
mid sweet long reddish hairs,
goes stiff and frantic with shame
and sates its wildest fancies there,

then slowly licks the balls, the land
'twixt scrotum and anus, races
up and down the magic wand,
pausing at the glans's base.

There, in search of bliss supreme,
greedy tongue teases out of
the spout an avalanche of cream
curdled on the cheese tray of love.

Next, after the customary
courtesies to the pisshole,
tongue returns to mouth very
hotly pursued by a blessed tool

overflowing with come which I
guzzle, anointed through friction,
amidst the peerless ecstasy
of this sacred benediction!

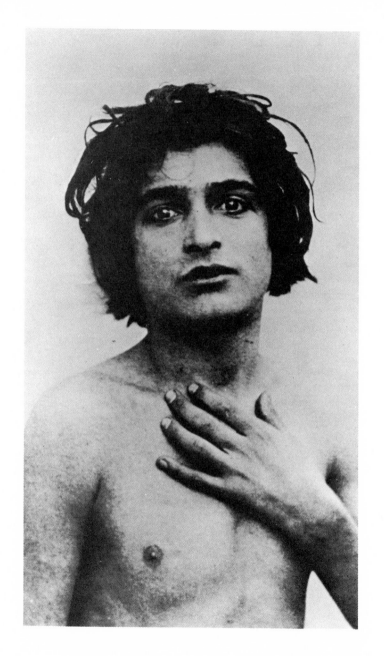

84

IX

He's a savage boy and every minute with him
gives me joy since he's the proud victim
and eager messmate of our perfect sleep
free of wet dreams—no need to?—and miscounted
    sheep,
he's so close to me I'd swear he's puckering up,
    as it were, waving his rod big with jelly
    over my quivering thighs and my belly.
One moment we're face to face, he turns around
like a good bread simmering till it's brown,
maybe his ass is delightfully dreamy,
blunt, saucy, sly, stubborn, whorish; creamy
motherfucker ass—fondled yet!—pokes my middle
aggressively and makes me potent as a devil,
or else I'll roll over sporting a shy crack
hot to get reamed, or we're back to back
and his rough but kind apathy glues our rumps
and my glad cock spritzes, then slumps,
hardens again and shoots, in endless repetition.
Am I happy? All of me's in a swell position!

X

Of course a woman's at her best
when screwing in her negligee;
of course your woman will protest
that it only feels okay

hidden as if by a veil
outlining all she's got—
thighs, calves, tits, ass,
and a big, gaping twat.

She will part her dainty shift
only when her holy snatch
needs a fuck or a lick—
and that's the end of the match.

Taking this cunt's full measure,
let's be frank and confess
she's too white, too pink
and her figure is a mess.

So a young man's better off
with some handsome male brute
whom he balls stark naked,
priest of Eros or recruit.

Behold his ravishing form,
so vibrant, so sensible,
heroic even if bashful,
and—a feature visible

in any torso, female
or even animal—o yes!—
the hypnotic grace of flesh
rippling in loveliness,

the play of muscle and bone,
firm pulp, lissome skin
obeying as it calls forth
every wild erotic whim,

body erect with passion,
alternately tense and lax,
to give and take pleasure
hard, then limp, in loving acts.

And when death at last shall smite
this virile form, to me divine,
in blue marble its majestic
features will forever shine.

XI

Even when it's not full-sized
your cock is my special treat
sprouting gold-white on your balls,
somber bait between your thighs.

My sweetheart's balls, pink and brown
and lavender proud sisters
afloat in their rawhide sack,
balls itching to fight and to clown.

The left one hangs with a sham-
saintly craftiness just
a little lower than the other,
but no one's fooled, goddamn!

Your prick's velvety and plump
from your groin down to the pink
crest of foreskin that dams
three-fourths of the gushing pump.

Swollen a bit at the tip,
beneath smooth skin it shows
the glans, fat as your nose,
barely protruding its lip.

After kisses a thousandfold
with loving gratitude my hand
lingers to fondle your gland
then grabs it with a firm hold

pulling the lace curtains back
till your delicate purple
glad cock, past holding out,
magnificently shoots its stack.

And then Bare-Headed-John
really steps on the gas,
fine bloke, and in a flash
all his limpness is gone.

You're big and hard, which satisfies
my mouth and my ass! Choose, master.
A simple jerk-off, maybe?
My ten-fingered exercise.

Meanwhile, your hallowed rod
proffers to my hands, lips, ass
(for worship in the high mass)
its exquisite form like a god.

XII

In this café packed with half-wits, the two of us
were the sole embodiments of the so-called monstrous
vice of "liking men," and while they sat unawares
we'd screw those cunts with their good-natured airs,
their bogus morals and conventional lusts.
Meanwhile, jiggering cut and thrust
galore, yet never unruly or obscene,
hidden by our pipes' misty smokescreen
(as when Hero balled Zeus in days of old),
our pricks, like Turkish shadow puppets' merry noses,
wiped by our hands with exquisite motion,
sneezed under the table fresh spurts of love-potion.

INNOCENT VERSES

O memory of infancy and the wet nurse's milk!
O the luxurious flights of adolescence!
When I was a wee boy, to conjure
up Woman and soothe the bitter pain
of having just one prick (a barely visible
stump beneath whose huge foreskin
all sperm to come, O sebaceous terror, lay in wait)
I'd regularly shoot off by dreaming of
nursie's velvet-smooth Mount of Venus.

Ever since, I draw my lace curtains and diddle my
        penis!

XIV

O my lovers,
   simple, swell cocks
   but with such tempers!
So comfort me for my hard knocks.
Your fine words will get my rocks off:
You, city punk, let's jerk off slangwise.
   You, country bumpkin, drawl in cocky language
of doggies in buns and stalks sweet to suck.
   In the thick woods let's join
      the great ruckus
      of tenderloin.
You, smart fops, let's tastefully go down
      and shit on the gloomy sermons
         of cunts and prudish dopes.
      (By cunts, I mean dummies
      cause the other cunts bewitch
      even us, the hard to please,
the elect, brothers of the good Church
      which has Plato for a pope
      and for a prothonotary Socrates.
A woman now and then is good form
and concessions never did any harm.
   Besides, to each his own, as they say,
and women, goodness knows, deserve their day.
      Take time from vice
      to do them nice
         then back to our oral play.)
   O my darling boys, avenge me
      through your earnest strokes

93

and the royal feast of your tools and behinds
        on all this hollow meat
which phrasemongers spawn in the shit-smeared minds
of our sorry pals who're fucking blind.
        No more metaphors: let's fuck.
        Let's jostle our balls a bit,
        cleanse our cocks, and feast
on come and asses and thighs and shit.

SONNET TO THE ASSHOLE*

Like a mauve carnation puckered up and dim
it breathes, meekly nestled amid the foam,
damp, too, from caresses tracing the smooth dome
of creamy buttocks up to the innermost rim.

Filaments oozing like drops of milk, driven
by the pitiless south wind, are blown
back across the russet marl's small stones
to vanish where the white slope sucks them in.

My mouth mates often with this air hole.
Jealous of this carnal union, my soul
fashions its nest of musky tears and sobs.

It's the drunken olive, the cajoling flute,
the heavenly praline's earthward chute,
feminine Canaan mid come bursting in gobs.

*The first two stanzas attributed to Verlaine, the last two
stanzas to Rimbaud

Oeuvres
Libres

AMIES

FEMMES

HOMBRES

Amies

SUR LE BALCON

Toutes deux regardaient s'enfuir les hirondelles:
L'une pâle aux cheveux de jais, et l'autre blonde
Et rose, et leurs peignoirs légers de vieille blonde
Vaguement serpentaient, nuages, autour d'elles.

Et toutes deux, avec des langueurs d'asphodèles,
Tandis qu'au ciel montait la lune molle et ronde,
Savouraient à longs traits l'émotion profonde
Du soir et le bonheur triste des coeurs fidèles.

Telles, leurs bras pressant, moites, leurs tailles
        souples,
Couple étrange qui prend pitié des autres couples,
Telles, sur le balcon, rêvaient les jeunes femmes.

Derrière elles, au fond du retrait riche et sombre,
Emphatique comme un trône de mélodrames
Et plein d'odeurs, le Lit, défait, s'ouvrait dans
        l'ombre.

PENSIONNAIRES

L'une avait quinze ans, l'autre en avait seize;
Toutes deux dormaient dans la même chambre.
C'était par un soir très lourd de septembre:
Frêles, des yeux bleus, des rougeurs de fraises.

Chacune a quitté, pour se mettre à l'aise,
La fine chemise au frais parfum d'ambre.
La plus jeune étend les bras, et se cambre,
Et sa soeur, les mains sur ses seins, la baise,

Puis tombe à genoux, puis devient farouche
Et colle sa tête au ventre, et sa bouche
Plonge sous l'or blond, dans les ombres grises;

Et l'enfant, pendant ce temps-là, recense
Sur ses doigts mignons des valses promises,
Et, rose, sourit avec innocence.

PER AMICA SILENTIA

Les longs rideaux de blanche mousseline
Que la lueur pâle de la veilleuse
Fait fluer comme une vague opaline
Dans l'ombre mollement mystérieuse,

Les grands rideaux du grand lit d'Adeline
Ont entendu, Claire, ta voix rieuse,
Ta douce voix argentine et câline
Qu'une autre voix enlace, furieuse.

"Aimons, aimons!" disaient vos voix mêlées,
Claire, Adeline, adorables victimes
Du noble voeu de vos âmes sublimes.

Aimez, aimez! ô chères Esseulées,
Puisqu'en ces jours de malheur, vous encore,
Le glorieux Stigmate vous décore.

PRINTEMPS

Tendre, la jeune femme rousse,
Que tant d'innocence émoustille,
Dit à la blonde jeune fille
Ces mots, tout bas, d'une voix douce:

"Sève qui monte et fleur qui pousse,
Ton enfance est une charmille:
Laisse errer mes doigts dans la mousse
Où le bouton de rose brille,

"Laisse-moi, parmi l'herbe claire,
Boire les gouttes de rosée
Dont la fleur tendre est arrosée,—

"Afin que le plaisir, ma chère,
Illumine ton front candide
Comme l'aube l'azur timide."

ETE

Et l'enfant répondit, pâmée
Sous la fourmillante caresse
De sa pantelante maîtresse:
"Je me meurs, ô ma bien-aimée!

"Je me meurs; ta gorge enflammée
Et lourde me soûle et m'oppresse;
Ta forte chair d'où sort l'ivresse
Est étrangement parfumée;

"Elle a, ta chair, le charme sombre
Des maturités estivales—
Elle en a l'ambre, elle en a l'ombre;

"Ta voix tonne dans les rafales,
Et ta chevelure sanglante
Fuit brusquement dans la nuit lente.

SAPPHO

Furieuse, les yeux caves et les seins roides,
Sappho, que la langueur de son désir irrite,
Comme une louve court le long des grèves froides.

Elle songe à Phaon, oublieuse du Rite,
Et, voyant à ce point ses larmes dédaignées,
Arrache ses cheveux immenses par poignées;

Puis elle évoque, en des remords sans accalmies,
Ces temps où rayonnait, pure, la jeune gloire
De ses amours chantées en vers que la mémoire
De l'âme va redire aux vierges endormies:

Et voilà qu'elle abat ses paupières blêmies,
Et saute dans la mer où l'appelle la Moire—
Tandis qu'au ciel éclate, incendiant l'eau noire,
La pâle Séléné qui venge les Amies.

Femmes

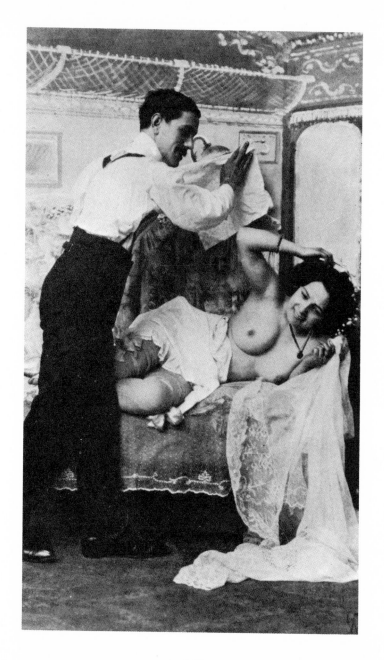

112

OUVERTURE

Je veux m'abstraire vers vos cuisses et vos fesses,
Putains, du seul vrai Dieu seules prêtresses vraies,
Beautés mûres ou non, novices ou professes,
O ne vivre plus qu'en vos fentes et vos raies!

Vos pieds sont merveilleux, qui ne vont qu'à l'amant,
Ne reviennent qu'avec l'amant, n'ont de répit
Qu'au lit pendant l'amour, puis flattent gentiment
Ceux de l'amant qui las et soufflant se tapit.

Pressés, fleurés, baisés, léchés depuis les plantes
Jusqu'aux orteils, sucés les uns après les autres,
Jusqu'aux chevilles, jusqu'aux lacs des veines lentes,
Pieds plus beaux que des pieds de héros et d'apôtres!

J'aime fort votre bouche et ses jeux gracieux,
Ceux de la langue et des lèvres et ceux des dents
Mordillant notre langue et parfois même mieux,
Trucs presque aussi gentils que de mettre dedans;

Et vos seins, double mont d'orgueil et de luxure,
Entre quels mon orgueil viril parfois se guinde
Pour s'y gonfler à l'aise et s'y frotter la hure:
Tel un sanglier ès vaux du Parnasse et du Pinde.

Vos bras! j'adore aussi vos bras si beaux, si blancs,
Tendres et durs, dodus, nerveux quand faut, et beaux
Et blancs comme vos culs et presque aussi troublants,
Chauds dans l'amour, après, frais comme des tom-
  beaux.

Et les mains au bout de ces bras, que je les gobe!
La caresse et la paresse les ont bénies,
Rameneuses du gland transi qui se dérobe,
Branleuses aux sollicitudes infinies!

Mais quoi! Tout ce n'est rien, Putains, aux prix de vos
Culs et cons dont la vue et le goût et l'odeur
Et le toucher font des élus de vos dévots,
Tabernacles et Saint des Saints de l'impudeur.

C'est pourquoi, mes soeurs, vers vos cuisses et vos
    fesses
Je veux m'abstraire tout, seules compagnes vraies,
Beautés mûres ou non, novices ou professes,
Et ne vivre plus qu'en vos fentes et vos raies.

A CELLE QUE L'ON DIT FROIDE

Tu n'es pas la plus amoureuse
De celles qui m'ont pris ma chair;
Tu n'es pas la plus savoureuse
De mes femmes de l'autre hiver.

Mais je t'adore tout de même!
D'ailleurs, ton corps doux et bénin
A tout, dans son calme suprême,
De si grassement féminin,

De si voluptueux sans phase,
Depuis les pieds longtemps baisés
Jusqu'à ces yeux clairs purs d'extase,
Mais que bien et mieux apaisés!

Depuis les jambes et les cuisses
Jeunettes sous la jeune peau,
A travers ton odeur d'éclisses,
Et d'écrevisses fraîches, beau.

Mignon, discret, doux petit Chose
A peine ombré d'un or fluet,
T'ouvrant en une apothéose
A mon désir rauque et muet,

Jusqu'aux jolis tétins d'infante,
De miss à peine en puberté,
Jusqu'à ta gorge triomphante
Dans sa gracile vénuste,

Jusqu'à ces épaules luisantes,
Jusqu'à la bouche, jusqu'au front
Naïfs aux mines innocentes
Qu'au fond les faits démentiront,

Jusqu'aux cheveux courts bouclés comme
Les cheveux d'un joli garçon,
Mais dont le flot nous charme, en somme,
Parmi leur apprêt sans façon,

En passant par la lente échine
Dodue à plaisir, jusques au
Cul somptueux, blancheur divine,
Rondeurs dignes de ton ciseau,

Mol Canova! jusques aux cuisses
Qu'il sied de saluer encor,
Jusqu'aux mollets, fermes délices,
Jusqu'aux talons de rose et d'or!—

Nos noeuds furent incoercibles?
Non, mais eurent leur attrait, leur.
Nos feux se trouvèrent terribles?
Non, mais donnèrent leur chaleur.

Quant au Point, Froide? Non pas, Fraîche.
Je dis que notre ''sérieux''
Fut surtout, et je m'en pourlèche,
Une masturbation mieux,

Bien qu'aussi bien les prévenances
Sussent te préparer sans plus—
Comme tu dis—d'inconvenances,
Pensionnaire qui me plut,

Et je te garde entre mes femmes
Du regret, non sans quelque espoir
De quand peut-être nous aimâmes
Et de sans doute nous r'avoir.

PARTIE CARREE

Chute des reins, chute du rêve enfantin d'être sage,
  Fesses, trône adoré de l'impudeur,
Fesses, dont la blancheur divinise encor la rondeur,
Triomphe de la chair mieux que celui par le visage!

Seins, double mont d'azur et de lait aux deux cîmes brunes
  Commandant quel vallon, quel bois sacré!
Seins, dont les bouts charmants sont un fruit vivant, savouré
Par la langue et la bouche ivre de ces bonnes fortunes!

Fesses, et leur ravin mignard d'ombre rose un peu sombre
  Où rôde le désir devenu fou,
Chers oreillers, coussins au pli profond pour la face ou
Le sexe, et frais repos des mains après ces tours sans nombre!

Seins, fins régals des mains qu'ils gorgent de délices,
  Seins lourds, puissants, un brin fiers et moqueurs,
Dandinés, balancés, et, se sentant forts et vainqueurs,
Vers nos prosternements comme regardant en coulisse!

Fesses, les grandes soeurs des seins vraiment, mais plus
    nature,
  Plus bonhomme, sourieuses aussi,
Mais sans malices trop et qui s'abstiennent du souci
De dominer, étant belles pour toute dictature!

Mais quoi? Vous quatre, bons tyrans, despotes doux et
   justes,
   Vous impériales et vous princiers,
Qui courbez le vulgaire et sacrez vos initiés,
Gloire et louange à vous, Seins très saints, Fesses très
   augustes!

TRIOLET A UNE VERTU
POUR S'EXCUSER DU PEU

A la grosseur du sentiment
Ne va pas mesurer ma force,
Je ne prétends aucunement
A la grosseur du sentiment.
Toi, serre le mien bontément
Entre ton arbre et ton écorce.
A la grosseur du sentiment
Ne va pas mesurer ma force.

La qualité vaut mieux, dit-on,
Que la quantité, fût-ce énorme.
Vive un gourmet, fi du glouton!
La qualité vaut mieux, dit-on.
Allons, sois gentille et que ton
Goût à ton désir se conforme.
La qualité vaut mieux, dit-on,
Que la quantité, fût-ce énorme.

Petit poisson deviendra grand
Pourvu que L'on lui prête vie.
Sois ce L'on-là; sur ce garant
Petit poisson deviendra grand,
Prête-la moi, je te le rend.—
Rai gaillard et digne d'envie.
Petit poisson deviendra grand
Pourvu que L'on lui prête vie.

Mon cas se rit de ton orgueil,
Etant fier et de grand courage.
Tu peux bien en faire ton deuil.
Mon cas se rit de ton orgueil
Comme du chat qui n'a qu'un oeil,
Et le voue au "dernier outrage."
Mon cas se rit de ton orgueil
Etant fier et de grand courage.

Tout de même et sans trop de temps
C'est fait. Sat prata. *L'ordre règne.*
Sabre au clair et tambours battants
Tout de même et sans trop de temps!
Bien que pourtant, bien que contents
Mon cas pleure et ton orgueil saigne.
Tout de même et sans trop de temps
C'est fait. Sat prata. *L'ordre règne.*

122

124

GOUTS ROYAUX

Louis Quinze aimait peu les parfums. Je l'imite
Et je leur acquiesce en la juste limite.
Ni flacons, s'il vous plaît, ni sachets en amour!
Mais, ô qu'un air naïf et piquant flotte autour
D'un corps, pourvu que l'art de m'exciter s'y trouve;
Et mon désir chérit et ma science approuve
Dans la chair convoitée, à chaque nudité,
L'odeur de la vaillance et de la puberté
Ou le relent très bon des belles femmes mûres.
Même j'adore—tais, morale, tes murmures—
Comment dirais-je? ces fumets, qu'on tient secrets,
Du sexe et des entours, dès avant comme après
La divine accolade et pendant la caresse,
Quelle qu'elle puisse être, ou doive, ou le paraisse.
Puis, quand sur l'oreiller mon odorat lassé,
Comme les autres sens, du plaisir ressassé,
Somnole et que mes yeux meurent vers un visage
S'éteignant presque aussi, souvenir et présage
De l'entrelacement des jambes et des bras,
Des pieds roux se baisant dans la moiteur des draps,
De cette langueur mieux voluptueuse monte
Un goût d'humanité qui ne va pas sans honte,
Mais si bon, mais si bon qu'on croirait en manger!
Dès lors, voudrais-je encor du poison étranger,
D'une fragrance prise à la plante, à la bête
Qui vous tourne le coeur et vous brûle la tête,
Puisque j'ai, pour magnifier la volupté,
Proprement la quintessence de la beauté!

FILLES I

Bonne simple fille des rues,
Combien te préféré-je aux grues

Qui nous encombrent le trottoir
De leur traîne, mon décrottoir,

Poseuses et bêtes poupées
Rien que de chiffons occupées

Ou de courses et de paris,
Fléaux déchaînés sur Paris!

Toi, tu m'es un vrai camarade
Qui la nuit monterait en grade.

Et même dans des draps câlins
Garderait des airs masculins,

Amante à la bonne franquette,
L'amie à travers la coquette

Qu'il te faut bien être un petit
Pour agacer mon appétit.

Oui, tu possèdes des manières
Si farceusement garçonnières

Qu'on croit presque faire un péché
(Pardonné puisqu'il est caché),

Sinon que t'as les fesses blanches,
De frais bras ronds et d'amples hanches

Et remplaces ce que n'as pas
Par tant d'orthodoxes appas.

T'es un copain tant t'es bonne âme.
Tant t'es toujours tout feu, tout flamme

S'il s'agit d'obliger les gens
Fût-ce avec tes pauvres argents

Jusqu'à doubler ta rude ouvrage,
Jusqu'à mettre du linge en gage!

Comme nous, t'as eu des malheurs
Et tes larmes valent nos pleus,

Et tes pleurs mêlés à nos larmes
Ont leurs salaces et leurs charmes.

Et de cette pitié que tu
Nous portes sort une vertu.

T'es un frère qu'est une dame
Et qu'est pour le moment ma femme . . .

Bon! puis dormons jusqu'à potron-
Minette, en boule, et ron, ron, ron!

Serre-toi, que je m'acoquine
Le ventre au bas de ton échine,

Mes genoux emboîtant les tiens,
Tes pieds de gosse entre les miens.

Roule ton cul sous ta chemise,
Mais laisse ma main que j'ai mise

Au chaud sous ton gentil tapis.
Là! nous voilà cois, bien tapis.

Ce n'est pas la paix, c'est la trêve.
Tu dors? Oui, pas de mauvais rêve.

Et je somnole en gais frissons,
Le nez pâmé sur tes frisons.

129

FILLES II

Et toi, tu me chausses aussi,
Malgré ta manière un peu rude
Qui n'est pas celle d'une prude
Mais d'un virago réussi.

Qui, tu me bottes quoique tu
Gargarises dans ta voix d'homme
Toutes les gammes du rogomme,
Buveuse à coude rabattu!

Mais femme! sacré nom de Dieu!
A nous faire perdre la tête,
Nous foutre tout le reste en fête
Et, nom de Dieu, le sang en feu.

Ton corps dresse, sous le reps noir,
Sans qu'assurément tu nous triches,
Une paire de nénés riches,
Souples, durs, excitants, faut voir!

Et moule un ventre jusqu'au bas,
Entre deux friands hauts-de-cuisse,
Qui parle de sauce et d'épice
Pour quel poisson de quel repas?

Tes bas blancs—et je t'applaudis
De n'arlequiner point tes formes—
Nous font ouvrir des yeux énormes
Sur des mollets que rebondis!

Ton visage de brune où les
Traces de robustes fatigues
Marquent clairement que tu briques
Surtout le choc des mieux râblés,

Ton regard ficelle et gobeur
Qui sait se mouiller puis qui mouille,
Qù toute la godaille grouille
Sans reproche, ô non! mais sans peur,

Toute ta figure—des pieds
Cambrés vers toutes les étreintes
Aux traits crépis, aux mêches teintes,
Par nos longs baisers épiés—

Ravigote les roquentins,
Et les ci-devant jeunes hommes
Que voilà bientôt que nous sommes,
Nous électrise en vieux pantins,

Fait de nous de vrais bacheliers,
Empressés autour de ta croupe,
Humant la chair comme une soupe,
Prête à râler sous tes souliers!

Tu nous mets bientôt à quia,
Mais, patiente avec nos restes,
Les accommodes, mots et gestes,
En ragoûts où de tout y a.

Et puis, quoique mauvaise au fond,
Tu nous as de ces indulgences!
Toi, si teigne entre les engeances,
Tu fais tant que les choses vont.

Tu nous gobes (ou nous le dis)
Non de te satisfaire, ô goule!
Mais de nous tenir à la coule
D'au moins les trucs les plus gentils.

Ces devoirs nous les déchargeons,
Parce qu'au fond tu nous violes,
Quitte à te fiche de nos fioles
Avec de plus jeunes cochons.

A MADAME ———

Quand tu m'enserres de tes cuisses
La tête ou les cuisses, gorgeant
Ma gueule des bathes délices
De ton jeune foutre astringent,

Ou mordant d'un con à la taille
Juste de tel passe-partout
Mon vit point très gros, mais canaille
Depuis les couilles jusqu'au bout,

Dans la pinette et la minette
Tu tords ton cul d'une façon
Qui n'est pas d'une femme honnête;
Et, nom de Dieu, t'as bien raison!

Tu me fais des langues fourrées,
Quand nous baisons, d'une longueur,
Et d'une ardeur démesurées
Qui me vont, merde! au droit du coeur,

Et ton con exprime ma pine
Comme un ours tetterait un pis,
Ours bien léché, toison rupine,
Que la mienne a pour fier tapis.

Ours bien léché, gourmande et soûle
Ma langue ici peut l'attester
Qui fit à ton clitoris boule-
De-gomme à ne le plus compter.

Bien léché, oui, mais âpre en diable,
Ton con joli, taquin, coquin,
Qui rit rouge sur le fond de sable:
Telles les lèvres d'Arlequin.

VAS UNGUENTATUM

Admire la brèche moirée
Et le ton rose-blanc qu'y met
La trace encor de mon entrée
Au Paradis de Mahomet.

Vois, avec un plaisir d'artiste,
O mon vieux regard fatigué
D'ordinaire à bon droit si triste,
Ce spectacle opulent et gai,

Dans un mol écrin de peluche
Noire aux reflets de cuivre roux
Qui serpente comme une ruche,
D'un bijou, le dieu des bijoux,

Palpitant de sève et de vie
Et vers l'extase de l'amant
Essorant la senteur ravie,
On dirait, à chaque élément.

Surtout contemple, et puis respire
Et finalement baise encor
Et toujours la gemme en délire,
Le rubis qui rit, fleur du for

Intérieur, tout petit frère
Epris de l'autre et le baisant
Aussi souvent qu'il peut le faire,
Comme lui soufflant à présent . . .

Mais repose-toi car tu flambes.
Aussi, lui, comment s'apaiser,
Cuisses et ventre, seins et jambes
Qui ne cessez de l'embraser?

Hélas! voici que son ivresse
Me gagne et s'en vient embrasser
Toute ma chair qui se redresse . . .
Allons, c'est à recommencer!

IDYLLE HIGH-LIFE

La galopine
A pleine main
Branle la pine
Au beau gamin.

L'heureux potache
Décalotté
Jouit et crache
De tous côtés.

L'enfant, rieuse,
A voir ce lait
Et curieuse
De ce qu'il est,

Hume une goutte
Au bord du pis,
Puis dame! en route,
Ma foi, tant pis!

Pourlèche et baise
Le joli bout,
Plus ne biaise,
Pompe le tout!

Petit vicomte
De Je-ne-sais,
Point ne raconte
Trop ce succès,

Fleur d'élégances,
Oaristys
De tes vacances
Quatre-vingt-dix:

Ces algarades
Dans les châteaux,
Tes camarades,
Même lourdeaux.

Pourraient sans peine
T'en raconter
A la douzaine
Sans inventer;

Et les cousines
Anges déchus,
De ces cuisines
Et de ces jus.

Sont coutumières,
Pauvres trognons,
Dès leurs premières
Communions:

Ce, jeunes frères,
En attendant
Leurs adultères
Vous impendant.

TABLEAU POPULAIRE

L'apprenti point trop maigrelet, quinze ans, pas beau,
Gentil dans sa rudesse un peu molle, la peau
Mate, l'oeil vif et creux, sort de sa cotte bleue,
Fringante et raide au point, sa déjà grosse queue
Et pine la patronne, une grosse encor bien,
Pâmée au bord du lit dans quel maintien vaurien,
Jambes en l'air et seins au clair, avec un geste!
A voir le gars serrer les fesses sous sa veste
Et les fréquents pas en avant que ses pieds font,
Il appert qu'il n'a pas peur de planter profond
Ni d'enceinter la bonne dame qui s'en fiche,
(Son cocu n'est-il pas là confiant et riche?).
Aussi bien, arrivée au suprême moment,
Elle s'écrie en un subit ravissement:
"Tu m'as fait un enfant, je le sens, et t'en aime
D'autant plus."—"Et voilà les bonbons du baptême!"
Dit-elle, après la chose; et tendre, à croppetons,
Lui soupèse et pelote et baise les roustons.

BILLET A LILY

Ma petite compatriote,
M'est avis que veniez ce soir
Frapper à ma porte et me voir.
O la scandaleuse ribote
De gros baisers—et de petits,
Conforme à mes gros appétits!
Mais les vôtres sont-ils si mièvres?
Primo, je baiserai vos lèvres,
Toutes! C'est mon cher entremets
Et les manières que j'y mets,
Comme en toutes choses vécues,
Sont friandes et convaincues.
Vous passerez vos doigts jolis
Dans ma flave barbe d'apôtre,
Et je caresserai la vôtre,
Et sur votre gorge de lys,
Où mes ardeurs mettront des roses,
Je poserai ma bouche en feu;
Mes bras se piqueront au jeu,
Pâmés autour des bonnes choses
De dessous la taille et plus bas,—
Puis mes mains, non sans fols combats
Avec vos mains mal courroucées,
Flatteront de tendres fessées
Ce beau derrière qu'étreindra
Tout l'effort qui lors bandera
Ma gravité vers votre centre . . .
A mon tour je frappe. O dis: Entre!

POUR RITA

J'abomine une femme maigre,
Pourtant je t'adore, ô Rita,
Avec tes lèvres un peu nègre
Où la luxure s'empâta,

Avec tes noirs cheveux, obscènes
A force d'être beaux ainsi,
Et tes yeux où ce sont des scènes
Sentant, parole! le roussi,

Tant leur feu sombre et gai quand même
D'une si lubrique gaîté
Eclaire de grâce suprême
Dans la pire impudicité,

Regard flûtant au virtuose
Es-pratiques dont on se tait:
"Quoi que tu te proposes, ose
Tout ce que ton cul te dictait";

Et sur ta taille comme d'homme,
Fine et très fine cependant,
Ton buste, perplexe Sodome
Entreprenant puis hésitant,

Car dans l'étoffe trop tendue
De tes corsages corrupteurs
Tes petits seins durs de statue
Disent: "Homme ou femme?" aux bandeurs.

Mais tes jambes, que féminines
Leur grâce grasse vers le haut
Jusques aux fesses que devine
Mon désir, jamais en défaut,

Dans les plis cochons de ta robe
Qu'un art salop sut disposer
Pour montrer plus qu'il ne dérobe
Un ventre où le mien se poser!

Bref, tout ton être ne respire
Que faims et soifs et passions . . .
Or je me crois encore pire:
Faudrait que nous comparassions.

Allons, vite au lit, mon infante,
Çà, livrons-nous jusqu'au matin
Une bataille triomphante
A qui sera le plus putain.

144

AU BAL

Un rêve de cuisses de femmes
Ayant pour ciel et pour plafond
Les culs et les cons de ces dames
Très beaux, qui viennent et qui vont.

Dans un ballon de jupes gaies
Sur des airs gentils et cochons;
Et les culs vous ont de ces raies,
Et les cons vous ont des manchons!

Des bas blancs sur quels mollets fermes
Si rieurs et si bandatifs
Avec, en haut, sans fins ni termes,
Ce train d'appâts en pendentifs,

Et des bottines bien cambrées
Moulant des pieds grands juste assez
Mènent des danses mesurées
En pas vifs, comme un peu lassés.

Une sueur particulière
Sentant à la fois bon et pas,
Foutre et mouille, et trouduculière,
Et haut de cuisse, et bas de bas,

Flotte et vire, joyeuse et molle,
Mêlée à des parfums de peau
A nous rendre la tête folle
Que les youtres ont sans chapeau.

Notez combien bonne ma place
Se trouve dans ce bal charmant:
Je suis par terre, et ma surface
Semble propice apparemment

Aux appétissantes danseuses
Qui veulent bien, on dirait pour
Telles intentions farceuses,
Tournoyer sur moi, quand mon tour,

Ce, par un extraordinaire
Privilège en elles ou moi,
Sans me faire mal, au contraire!
Car l'aimable, le doux émoi

Que ces cinq cent mille chatouilles
De petons vous caracolant
A même les jambes, les couilles,
Le ventre, la queue et le gland!

Les chants se taisent et les danses
Cessent. Aussitôt les fessiers
De mettre au pas leurs charmes denses.
O ciel! l'un d'entre eux, tu t'assieds

Juste sur ma face, de sorte
Que ma langue entre les deux trous
Divins, vague de porte en porte
Au pourchas de riches ragoûts.

Tous les derrières à la file
S'en viennent généreusement
M'apporter, chacun en son style,
Ce vrai banquet d'un vrai gourmand.

Je me réveille, je me touche;
C'est bien moi, le pouls au galop . . .
Le nom de Dieu de fausse couche!
Le nom de Dieu de vrai salop!

REDDITION

Je suis foutu. Tu m'as vaincu.
Je n'aime plus que ton gros cu
Tant baisé, léché, reniflé,
Et que ton cher con tant branlé,
Piné—car je ne suis pas l'homme
Pour Gomorrhe ni pour Sodome,
Mais pour Paphos et pour Lesbos,
(Et tant gamahuché, ton con),
Converti par tes seins si beaux,
Tes seins lourds que mes mains soupèsent
Afin que mes lèvres les baisent
Et, comme l'on hume un flacon,
Sucent leurs bouts raides, puis mous,
Ainsi qu'il nous arrive à nous
Avec nos gaules variables.
C'est un plaisir de tous les diables
Que tirer un coup en gamin,
En épicier ou en levrette,
Ou à la Marie-Antoinette
Et caetera jusqu'à demain
Avec toi, despote adorée,
Dont la volonté m'est sacrée,
Plaisir infernal qui me tue

Et dans lequel je m'exténue
A satisfaire ta luxure.
Le foutre s'épand de mon vit
Comme le sang d'une blessure . . .
N'importe! Tant que mon coeur vit
Et que palpite encor mon être,
Je veux remplir en tout ta loi,
N'ayant, dure maîtresse, en toi
Plus de maîtresse, mais un maître.

REGALS

Croise tes cuisses sur ma tête
De façon à ce que ma langue,
Taisant toute sotte harangue,
Ne puisse plus que faire fête
A ton con ainsi qu'à ton cu
Dont je suis l'à-jamais vaincu
Comme de tout ton corps, du reste,
Et de ton âme mal céleste,
Et de ton esprit carnassier
Qui dévore en moi l'idéal
Et m'a fait le plus putassier
Du plus pur, du plus lilial
Que j'étais avant ta rencontre
Depuis des ans et puis des ans.
Là, dispose-toi bien et montre
Par quelques gestes complaisants
Qu'au fond t'aime ton vieux bonhomme
Ou du moins le souffre faisant
Minette (avec boule de gomme)
Et feuille de rose, tout comme
Un plus jeune mieux séduisant
Sans doute, mais moins bath en somme
Quant à la science et au faire.
O ton con! qu'il sent bon! J'y fouille
Tant de la gueule que du blaire
Et j'y fais le diable et j'y flaire
Et j'y farfouille et j'y bafouille
Et j'y renifle et oh! J'y bave
Dans ton con à l'odeur cochonne

Que surplombe une motte flave
Et qu'un duvet roux environne
Qui mène au trou miraculeux,
Qù je farfouille, où je bafouille,
Qù je renifle et où je bave
Avec le soin méticuleux
Et l'âpre ferveur d'un esclave
Affranchi de tout préjugé.
La raie adorable que j'ai
Léchée amoroso depuis
Les reins en passant par le puits
Où je m'attarde en un long stage
Pour les dévotions d'usage,
Me conduit tout droit à la fente
Triomphante de mon infante.
Là, je dis un salamalec
Absolument ésotérique
Au clitoris rien moins que sec,
Si bien que ma tête d'en bas
Qu'exaspèrent tous ces débats
S'épanche en blanche rhétorique,
Mais s'apaise dès ces prémisses.

Et je m'endors entre tes cuisses
Qu'à travers tout cet émoi tendre
La fatigue t'a fait détendre.

GAMINERIES

Depuis que ce m'est plus commode
De baiser en gamin, j'adore
Cette manière et l'aime encore
Plus quand j'applique la méthode

Qui consiste à mettre mes mains
Bien fort sur ton bon gros cul frais,
Chatouille un peu conçue exprès
Pour mieux entrer dans tes chemins.

Alors ma queue est en ribote
De ce con, qui, de fait, la baise,
Et de ce ventre qui lui pèse
D'un poids salop—et ça clapote,

Et les tétons de déborder
De la chemise lentement
Et de danser indolemment,
Et de mes yeux comme bander,

Tandis que les tiens, d'une vache,
Tels ceux-là des Junons antiques,
Leur fichent des regards obliques,
Profonds comme des coups de hache,

Si que je suis magnétisé
Et que mon cabochon d'en bas,
Non toutefois sans quels combats!
Se rend tout à fait médusé.

Et je jouis et je décharge
Dans ce vrai cauchemar de viande
A la fois friande et gourmande
Et tour à tour étroite et large,

Et qui remonte et redescend
Et rebondit sur mes roustons
En sauts où mon vit à tâtons
Pris d'un vertige incandescent

Parmi des foutres et des mouilles
Meurt, puis revit, puis meurt encore,
Revit, remeurt, revit encore
Par tout ce foutre et que de mouilles!

Cependant que mes doigts, non sans
Te faire un tas de postillons,
Légers comme des papillons
Mais profondément caressants,

Et que mes paumes, de tes fesses
Froides modérément tout juste,
Remontent **lento** *vers le buste*
Tiède sous leurs chaudes caresses.

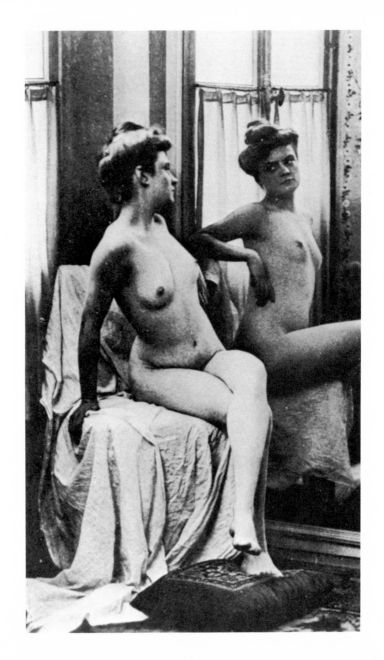

154

HOMMAGE DU

Je suis couché tout de mon long sur son lit frais:
Il fait grand jour; c'est plus cochon, plus fait exprès,
Par le prolongement dans la lumière crue
De la fête nocturne immensément accrue,
Pour la persévérance et la rage du cu
Et ce soin de se faire soi-même cocu.
Elle est à poils et s'accroupit sur mon visage
Pour se faire gamahucher, car je fus sage
Hier et c'est—bonne, elle, au-delà du penser!—
Sa royale façon de me récompenser.
Je dis royale, je devrais dire divine:
Ces fesses, chair sublime, alme peau, pulpe fine,
Galbe puissamment pur, blanc, riche, aux stries d'azur.
Cette raie au parfum bandatif, rose-obscur,
Lente, grasse, et le puits d'amour, que dire sur!
Régal final, dessert du con bouffé, délire
De ma langue harpant les plis comme une lyre!
Et ces fesses encor, telle une lune en deux
Quartiers, mystérieuse et joyeuse, où je veux
Dorénavant nicher mes rêves de poète
Et mon coeur de tendeur et mes rêves d'esthète!
Et, maîtresse, ou mieux, maître en silence obéi,
Elle trône sur moi, caudataire ébloui.

MORALE EN RACCOURCI

Une tête de blonde et de grâce pâmée,
Sous un cou roucouleur de beaux tétons bandants,
Et leur médaillon sombre à la mamme enflammée,
Ce buste assis sur des coussins bas, cependant
Qu'entre deux jambes, très vibrantes, très en l'air,
Une femme à genoux vers quels soins occupée—
Amour le sait—ne montre aux dieux que l'épopée
Candide de son cul splendide, miroir clair
De la Beauté qui veut s'y voir afin d'y croire.
Cul féminin, vainqueur serein du cul viril,
Fût-il éphébéen, et fût-il puéril.
Cul féminin, cul sur tous culs, los, culte et gloire!

Hombres

I

O ne blasphème pas, poète, et souviens-toi.
Certes la femme est bien, elle vaut qu'on la baise,
Son cul lui fait honneur, encor qu'un brin obèse,
Et je l'ai savouré maintes fois, quant à moi.

Ce cul (et les tétons), quel nid à nos caresses!
Je l'embrasse à genoux et lèche son pertuis
Tandis que mes doigts vont, fouillant dans l'autre puits,
Et les beaux seins, combien cochonnes leurs paresses!

Et puis, il sert, ce cul, encor, surtout au lit
Comme adjuvant aux fins de coussins, de sous-ventre,
De ressort à boudin du vrai ventre pour qu'entre
Plus avant l'homme dans la femme qu'il élit.

J'y délasse mes mains, mes bras aussi, mes jambes,
Mes pieds.—Tant de fraîcheur, d'élastique rondeur
M'en font un reposoir désirable où, rôdeur,
Par instants le désir sautille en voeux ingambes.

Mais comparer le cul de l'homme à ce bon cu!
A ce gros cul moins voluptueux que pratique,
Le cul de l'homme, fleur de joie et d'esthétique,
Surtout l'en proclamer le serf et le vaincu!

"C'est mal!" a dit l'Amour. Et la voix de l'Histoire:
Cul de l'homme, honneur pur de l'Hellade et décor
Divin de Rome vraie et plus divin encor
De Sodome morte, martyre pour sa gloire.

Shakspeare, abandonnant du coup Ophélia,
Cordélia, Desdémona, tout son beau sexe
Chantait en vers magnificents—qu'un sot s'en vexe—
La forme masculine et son alleluia.

Les Valois étaient fous du mâle et dans notre ère
L'Europe embourgeoisée et féminine tant
Néanmoins admira ce Louis de Bavière,
Le roi vierge au grand coeur pour l'homme seul battant.

La Chair, même la chair de la femme, proclame
Le cul, le vit, le torse et l'oeil du fier Puceau,
Et c'est pourquoi, d'après le conseil à Rousseau,
Il faut parfois, poète, un peu "quitter la dame."

MILLE E TRE

Mes amants n'appartiennent pas aux classes riches:
Ce sont des ouvriers faubouriens ou raraux,
Leurs quinze et leurs vingt ans sans apprêts, sont mal chiches
De force assez brutale et de procédés gros.

Je les goûte en habits de travail, cotte et veste;
Ils ne sentent pas l'ambre et fleurent de santé
Pure et simple; leur marche un peu lourde, va, preste
Pourtant, car jeune, et grave en l'élasticité;

Leurs yeux francs et matois crépitent de malice
Cordiale et des mots naïvement rusés
Partent—non sans un gai juron qui les épice—
De leur bouche bien fraîche aux solides baisers;

Leur pine vigoureuse et leurs fesses joyeuses
Réjouissent, la nuit et ma queue et mon cu;
Sous la lampe et le petit jour, leurs chairs joyeuses
Ressuscitent mon désir las, jamais vaincu.

Cuisses, âmes, mains, tout mon être pêle-mêle,
Mémoire, pieds, coeur, dos et l'oreille et le nez,
Et la fressure, tout gueule une ritournelle
Et trépigne un chahut dans leurs bras forcenés.

Un chahut, une ritournelle, fol et folle,
Et plutôt divins qu'infernals, plus infernals
Que divins, à m'y perdre, et j'y nage et j'y vole,
Dans leurs sueurs et leur haleine, dans ces bals.

Mes deux Charles: l'un, jeune tigre aux yeux de chatte,
Sorte d'enfant de choeur grandissant en soudard;
L'autre, fier gaillard, bel effronté que n'épate
Que ma pente vertigineuse vers son dard.

Odilon, un gamin, mais monté comme un homme,
Ses pieds aiment les miens épris de ses orteils
Mieux encor, mais pas plus que de son reste en somme
Adorable drûment, mais ses pieds sans pareils!

Caresseurs, satin frais, délicates phalanges
Sous les plantes, autour des chevilles, et sur
La cambrure veineuse, et ces baisers étranges
Si doux, de quatre pieds ayant une âme, sûr!

Antoine, encor proverbial quand à la queue,
Lui, mon roi triomphal et mon suprême Dieu,
Taraudant tout mon coeur de sa prunelle bleue,
Et tout mon cul de son épouvantable épieu;

Paul, un athlète blond aux pectoraux superbes,
Poitrine blanche, aux durs boutons sucés ainsi
Que le bon bout; François, souple comme des gerbes,
Ses jambes de danseur, et beau, son chibre aussi!

Auguste qui se fait de jour en jour plus mâle
(Il était bien joli quand ça nous arriva!);
Jules, un peu putain avec sa beauté pâle;
Henri, miraculeux conscrit qui, las! s'en va;

Et vous tous, à la file ou confondus, en bande
Ou seuls, vision si nette des jours passés,
Passions du présent, futur qui croît et bande,
Chéris sans nombre qui n'êtes jamais assez!

163

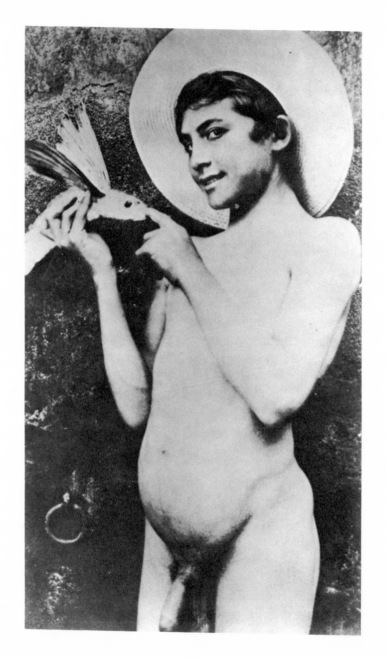

164

BALANIDE

I

C'est un plus petit coeur
Avec la pointe en l'air;
Symbole doux et fier,
C'est un plus tendre coeur.

Il verse ah! que de pleurs
Corrosifs plus que feu,
Prolongés mieux qu'adieu,
Blancs comme blanches fleurs!

Vêtu de violet,
Fait beau le voir yssir,
Mais à tout le plaisir
Qu'il donne quand lui plaît!

Comme un évêque au choeur
Il est plein d'onction.
Sa bénédiction
Va de l'autel au choeur.

Il ne met que du soir
Au réveil auroral
Son anneau pastoral
D'améthyste et d'or noir.

Puis le rite accompli,
Déchargé congrûment,
De ramener dûment
Son capuce joli.

II

Gland, point suprême de l'être
   De mon maître,
De mon amant adoré
Qu'accueille avec joie et crainte,
   Ton étreinte
Mon heureux cul, perforé

Tant et tant par ce gros membre
   Qui se cambre,
Se gonfle et, tout glorieux
De ces hauts faits et prouesses,
   Dans les fesses
Fonce en élans furieux.—

Nourricier de la fressure,
   Source sûre
Qù ma bouche aussi suça,
Gland, ma grande friandise,
   Quoi qu'en dise
Quelque fausse honte; or, ça,

Gland, mes délices, viens, dresse
  Ta caresse
De chaud satin violet
Qui dans ma main se harnache
  En panache
Soudain d'opale et de lait.

Ce n'est que pour une douce
  Sur le pouce
Que je t'invoque aujourd'hui;
Mais quoi! ton ardeur se fâche . . .
  O moi lâche!
Va, tout à toi, tout à lui!

Ton caprice, règle unique.
  Je rapplique
Pour la bouche et pour le cu,
Les voici tout prêts, en selle,
  D'humeur telle
Qu'il te faut, maître invaincu.

Puis, gland, nectar et dictame
  De mon âme,
Rentre en ton prépuce, lent
Comme un dieu dans son nuage.
  Mon hommage
T'y suit, fidèle—et galant.

SUR UNE STATUE

Eh quoi! Dans cette ville d'eaux,
Trêve, repos, paix, intermède,
Encor toi de face ou de dos
Beau petit ami Ganymède?

L'aigle t'emporte, on dirait comme
A regret, de parmi les fleurs,
Son aile, d'élans économe,
Semble te vouloir par ailleurs

Que chez ce Jupin tyrannique,
Comme qui dirait au Revard,
Et son oeil qui nous fait la nique
Te coule un drôle de regard.

Bah! reste avec nous, bon garçon,
Notre ennui, viens donc le distraire
Un peu de la bonne façon:
N'es-tu pas notre petit frère?

RENDEZ-VOUS

Dans la chambre encore fatale
De l'encor fatale maison
Où la raison et la morale
Se tiennent plus que de raison,

Il semble attendre la venue
A quoi, misère, il ne croit pas
De quelque présence connue
Et murmure entre haut et bas:

"Ta voix claironne dans mon âme
Et tes yeux flambent dans mon coeur.
Le monde dit que c'est infâme;
Mais que me fait, ô mon vainqueur!

"J'ai la tristesse et j'ai la joie,
Et j'ai l'amour encore un coup,
L'amour ricaneur qui larmoie,
O toi, beau comme un petit loup!

"Tu vins à moi, gamin farouche,
C'est toi—joliesse et bagou—
Rusé du corps et de la bouche,
Qui me violentes dans tout

"Mon scrupule envers ton extrême
Jeunesse et ton enfance mal
Encore débrouillée, et même
Presque dans tout mon animal.

"Deux, trois ans sont passés à peine,
Suffisants pour viriliser
Ta fleur d'alors et ton haleine
Encore prompte à s'épuiser.

"Quel rude gaillard tu dois être
Et que les instants seraient bons
Si tu pouvais venir! Mais, traître,
Tu promets, tu dis: J'en réponds.

"Tu jures le ciel et la terre,
Puis tu rates les rendez-vous . . .
Ah! cette fois, viens! Obtempère
A mes désirs qui tournent fous.

"Je t'attends comme le Messie,
Arrive, tombe dans mes bras;
Une rare fête choisie
Te guette, arrive, tu verras!"

Du phosphore en ses yeux s'allume
Et sa lèvre au souris pervers
S'agace aux barbes de la plume
Qu'il tient pour écrire ces vers . . .

VII

Monte sur moi comme une femme
Que je baiserais en gamin.
Là. C'est cela. T'es à ta main?
Tandis que mon vit t'entre, lame

Dans du beurre, du moins ainsi
Je puis te baiser sur la bouche,
Te faire une langue farouche
Et cochonne, et si douce, aussi!

Je vois tes yeux auxquels je plonge
Les miens, jusqu'au fond de ton coeur,
D'où mon désir revient vainqueur
Dans une luxure de songe.

Je caresse le dos nerveux,
Les flancs ardents et frais, la nuque,
La double mignonne perruque
Des aisselles et les cheveux!

Ton cul à cheval sur mes cuisses
Les pénètre de son doux poids
Pendant que s'ébat mon lourdois
Aux fins que tu te réjouisses.

Et tu te réjouis, petit,
Car voici que ta belle gaule,
Jalouse aussi d'avoir son rôle,
Vite, vite, gonfle, grandit,

Raidit . . . Ciel! la goutte, la perle
Avant-courrière, vient briller
Au méat rose: l'avaler,
Moi, je le dois, puisque déferle

Le mien de flux. Or c'est mon lot
De faire tôt d'avoir aux lèvres
Ton gland chéri tout lourd de fièvres
Qu'il décharge en un royal flot.

Lait suprême, divin phosphore
Sentant bon la fleur d'amandier,
Où vient l'âpre soif mendier
La soif de toi qui me dévore.

Mais il va, riche et généreux,
Le don de ton adolescence,
Communiant, de ton essence,
Tout mon être ivre d'être heureux.

VIII

Un peu de merde et de fromage
Ne sont pas pour effaroucher
Mon nez, ma bouche et mon courage
Dans l'amour de gamahucher.

L'odeur m'est assez gaie en somme,
Du trou du cul de mes amants,
Aigre et fraîche comme de pomme
Dans la moiteur de sains ferments.

Et ma langue que rien ne dompte,
Par la douceur des longs poils roux
Raide et folle de bonne honte,
Assouvit là ses plus forts goûts.

Puis pourléchant le périnée
Et les couilles d'un mode lent,
Au long du chibre contournée
S'arrête à la base du gland.

Elle y puise âprement, en quête
Du nanan qu'elle mourrait pour,
Sive la crème de quéquette
Caillée aux éclisses d'amour,

Ensuite, après la politesse
Traditionnelle au méat,
Rentre dans la bouche où s'empresse
De la suivre le vit béat,

Débordant de foutre qu'avale
Ce moi, confit en onction,
Parmi l'extase sans rivale
De cette bénédiction!

IX

Il est mauvais coucheur et ce m'est une joie
De le bien sentir, lorsqu'il est la fière proie
Et le fort commensal du meilleur des sommeils
Sans fausses couches—nul besoin?—et sans réveils,
Si près, si près de moi que je crois qu'il me baise,
   En quelque sorte, avec son gros vit que je sens
   Dans mes cuisses et sur mon ventre, frémissants.
Si nous nous trouvons face à face, et s'il se tourne
De l'autre côté, tel qu'un bon pain qu'on enfourne,
Son cul délicieusement rêveur ou non,
Soudain, mutin, malin, hutin, putain, son nom
De Dieu de cul, d'ailleurs choyé, m'entre en le ventre,
Provocateur et me rend bandeur comme un diantre,
Ou si je lui tourne le mien semble vouloir
M'enculer ou, si dos à dos, son nonchaloir
Brutal et gentil colle à mes fesses ses fesses,
Et mon vit de bonheur, tu mouilles, puis t'affaisses
Et rebande et remouille, infini dans cet us.
Heureux moi? "Totus in benigno positus!"

X

Autant certes la femme gagne
A faire l'amour en chemise,
Autant alors cette compagne
Est-elle seulement de mise

A la condition expresse
D'un voile, court, délinéant
Cuisse et mollet, téton et fesse
Et leur truc un peu trop géant,

Ne s'écartant de sorte nette,
Qu'en faveur du con, seul divin,
Pour le coup et pour la minette,
Et tout le reste, en elle, est vain.

A bien considérer les choses,
Ce manque de proportions,
Ces effets trop blancs et trop roses . . .
Faudrait que nous en convinssions,

Autant le jeune homme profite
Dans l'intérêt de sa beauté,
Prêtre d'Eros ou néophyte
D'aimer en toute nudité.

Admirons cette chair splendide,
Comme intelligente, vibrant,
Intrépide et comme timide
Et, par un privilège grand

Sur toute chair, la féminine
Et la bestiale—vrai beau!—
O cette grâce qui fascine
D'être multiple sous la peau,

Jeu des muscles et du squelette,
Pulpe ferme, souple tissu,
Elle interprète, elle complète
Tout sentiment soudain conçu.

Elle se bande en la colère,
Et raide et molle tour à tour,
Souci de se plaire et de plaire,
Se tend et détend dans l'amour.

Et, quand la mort la frappera,
Cette chair qui me fut un dieu,
Comme auguste, elle fixera
Ses éléments, en marbre bleu!

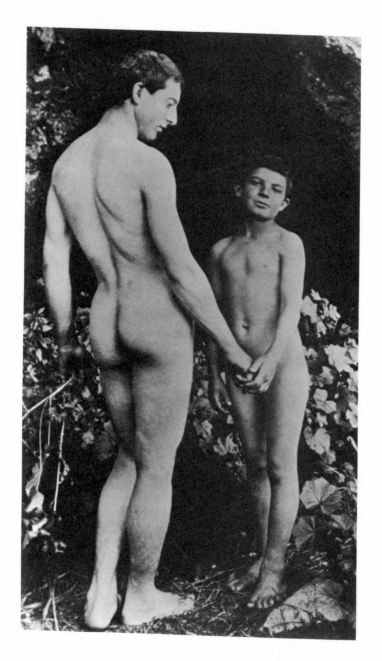

Même quand tu ne bandes pas,
Ta queue encor fait mes délices
Qui pend, blanc d'or entre tes cuisses,
Sur tes roustons, sombres appas.

—Couilles de mon amant, soeurs fières
A la riche peau de chagrin,
D'un brun et rose et purpurin,
Couilles farceuses et guerrières,

Et dont la gauche balle un peu
Tout petit peu plus bas que l'autre,
D'un air roublard et bon apôtre,
A quelles donc fins, nom de Dieu?—

Elle est dodue ta quéquette,
Et veloutée, du pubis
Au prépuce fermant le pis,
Aux trois quarts, d'une rose crête.

Elle se renfle un brin au bout
Et dessine sous la peau douce
Le gland gros comme un demi-pouce
Montrant ses lèvres juste au bout.

Après que je l'aurai baisée
En tout amour reconnaissant,
Laisse ma main, la caressant,
La saisir d'une prise osée,

Pour, soudain, la décalotter;
En sorte que, violet tendre,
Le gland joyeux, sans plus attendre,
Splendidement vienne éclater;

Et puis elle, en bonne bougresse,
Accélère le mouvement
Et Jean-nu-tête en un moment
De se remettre à la redresse.

Tu bandes! C'est ce que voulaient
Ma bouche et mon cul! choisis, maître.
Une simple douce, peut-être?
C'est ce que mes dix doigts voulaient.

Cependant le vit, mon idole,
Tend, pour le rite et pour le cul-
Te, à mes mains, ma bouche et mon cul
Sa forme adorable d'idole.

XIV

O mes amants,
Simples natures,
Mais quels tempéraments!
Consolez-moi de ces mésaventures.
Reposez-moi de ces littératures;
Toi, gosse pantinois, branlons-nous en argot,
Vous, gas des champs, patoisez-moi l'écot,
Des pines au cul et des plumes qu'on taille,
Livrons-nous dans les bois touffus
La grande bataille
Des baisers confus.
Vous, rupins, faisons des langues en artistes
Et merde aux discours tristes
Des pédants et des cons.
(Par cons, j'entends les imbéciles,
Car les autres cons sont de mise
Même pour nous, les difficiles,
Les spéciaux, les servants de la bonne Eglise
Dont le pape serait Platon
Et Socrate un protonotaire
Une femme par-ci par-là, c'est le bon ton
Et les concessions n'ont jamais rien perdu.
Puis, comme dit l'autre, à chacun son dû,
Et les femmes ont, mon dieu, droit à notre gloire.
Soyons-leur doux
Entre deux coups,
Puis, revenons à notre affaire.)
O mes enfants bien-aimés, vengez-moi
Par vos caresses sérieuses

Et vos culs et vos noeuds, régals vraiment de roi,
De toutes ces viandes creuses
Qu'offre la réthorique aux cervelles breneuses
De ces tristes copains qui ne savent pourquoi.
Ne métaphorons pas, foutons,
Pelotons-nous bien les roustons,
Rinçons nos glands, faisons ripailles
Et de foutre et de merde et de fesses et de cuisses.

LE SONNET DU TROU DU CUL

Obscur et froncé comme un oeillet violet
Il respire, humblement tapi parmi la mousse,
Humide encor d'amour qui suit la pente douce
Des fesses blanches jusqu'au bord de son ourlet.

Des filaments pareils à des larmes de lait
Ont pleuré, sous l'autan cruel qui les repousse,
A travers de petits cailloux de marne rousse,
Pour s'en aller où la pente les appelait.

Ma bouche s'accoupla souvent à sa ventouse,
Mon âme, du coit matériel jalouse,
En fit son larmier fauve et son nid de sanglots.

C'est l'olive pâmée et la flûte câline,
C'est le tube où descend la céleste praline,
Chanaan féminin dans les moiteurs éclos.

EDITOR'S NOTES

INTRODUCTION

1. Paul Verlaine, *Oeuvres Libres: Première édition critique, suivie de notes, de variantes, d'un essai de bibliographie, et précédé d'une introduction par Jissey* (Metz: Au Verger des Amours, 1949).

2. A. E. Carter, *Verlaine: A Study in Parallels* (Toronto: University of Toronto Press, 1969).

3. Antoine Adam, *Verlaine, l'homme et l'oeuvre* (Paris: Hatier-Boivin, 1953).

4. Marcel Coulon, *Verlaine, poète saturnien* (Paris: Grasset, 1929).

5. Antoine Adam, *Le vrai Verlaine. Essai psychanalytique* (Paris: Droz, 1936).

6. Lawrence and Elisabeth Hanson, *Verlaine: Fool of God* (New York: Random House, 1957).

7. A. E. Carter, *op. cit.*

8. Verlaine, *op. cit.*

9. Paul Verlaine, *Oeuvres poétiques complètes*, ed. Y.-G. Le Dantec, revised by Jacques Borel (Paris: Bibliothèque de la Pléiade, 1962).

POEMS

p. 11 Sappho
In Greek legend, Sappho jumps to her death off the Leucadian rock. She commits suicide in desperation at her unrequited love for Phaon, a ferryman of Lesbos endowed by Aphrodite with terrific good looks or a potent charm.

Stz. 4, l. 2   Selene (Si-lē'-nē) is the Greek moon goddess. She is usually represented as a woman with moonlike features driving a two-horse chariot.

p. 18 To one who is called frigid / A celle que l'on dit froide
Stz. 10   Antonio Canova (1757–1822), the Italian neoclassical sculptor, was noted for the grace and sensuality of his forms.

p. 23 Triolet to a virtuous woman / Triolet a une vertu . . .
Stz. 3   parodies La Fontaine's fable, *Le petit poisson et le pêcheur* (Livre V, Fable 3). The relevant lines are:

Petit poisson deviendra grand
Pourvu que Dieu lui prête vie.

Mais le lâcher en attendant,
Je tiens pour moi que c'est folie . . .

Stz. 5, l. 2 *Sat prata* echoes the close of Virgil's third *Eclogue,*
sat prata biberunt (III.111), which means, "The meadows have
drunk their fill," here a metaphor for consummated copulation.

p. 39 Perfumed dish / Vas unguentatum
Vas unguentatum is Latin for an anointed or perfumed dish or
vessel. The title probably refers also to the ducts and glands that
lubricate the female genitalia.

p. 46 Love note for Lily / Billet a Lily
l. 1 *compatriote* Lily may be Caroline Teisen, a prostitute who
was a native of Metz like Verlaine. She met the poet around 1886
and later went mad on learning of his death.

p. 60 Games with you on top / Gamineries
The pun of the title indicates that the mischievous pranks of
the poet and his bedmate are performed while they copulate *en*
gamin, i.e., with the conventional positions of man and woman
reversed.

p. 68 Hombres I
Stz. 8 Bisexuality and homosexuality flourished at the court
of the Valois dynasty, which reigned in France from 1328 to 1589.
King Ludwig II of Bavaria (1845–86), liberal, gifted, romantic,
a patron of the arts, was a cult figure among *fin de siècle* decadents.
His eccentric, mentally unbalanced nature found expression in
fantastical, ornate castles and other extravagant architectural
projects. His affairs with stableboys, actors, and officers were
bruited about. The last years of his life were marked by insanity
and seclusion, ending in suicide by drowning.

p. 71 Mille e tre
The poem burlesques the famous macho "Il Catalogo" aria in
Mozart's opera *Don Giovanni*. In this aria the Don's servant
Leporello enumerates his master's sexual conquests country by
country, culminating in the ritornello, "Ma in Ispagna . . . mille
e tre!" (But in Spain, one thousand and three women screwed.)

p. 73 Song of the prick / Balanide
The title, apparently a coinage of Verlaine's, is a play upon
ballade and *balane,* sexual argot for the penis with prepuce drawn
back.
l. 8 *Blanches fleurs* imitates *fleurs blanches,* meaning leukorrhea,
a whitish vaginal discharge.

p. 76 To a statue / Sur une statue

Ganymede, a beautiful Trojan youth, was abducted to Mount Olympus to be cupbearer and lover of Zeus (Jove or Jupiter in Roman mythology). In some versions of the myth, the boy was snatched up by an eagle which may have been Zeus himself. In other accounts he was carried off by a whirlwind.

l. 10   Revard is a mountain in the vicinity of Aix-les-Bains.

l. 16   *Petit frère* is one of the most common expressions in French for penis.

For details on the actual statue which inspired this poem, see *Oeuvres poétiques complètes* (Gallimard. Bibliothèque de la Pléiade, 1973, pp. 1212–13).

p. 90 Hombres XII

l. 9   Arthur Bernard Cook's monumental *Zeus: A Study in Ancient Religion* cites many of Zeus's extramarital affairs, but there is no mention of the lovely priestess Hero. Perhaps *Héro* is a misprint for Zeus's wife Hera, or Verlaine may be engaging in mythmaking.

l. 10   *Karragheus Karagöz*, the Turkish shadow play or puppet theater, spread to Europe in the seventeenth century and was a popular entertainment in Paris in Verlaine's time. Karagöz, the leading character, whose name means "Black Eye," is a witty and vulgar fellow distinguished by his huge member.

p. 92 Innocent verses / Dizain ingenu

A *dizain* is a ten-line stanza.

p. 93 Hombres XIV

l. 6   *pantinois* A resident of Pantin, a northeastern industrial suburb of Paris.

p. 96 Sonnet to the asshole / Le sonnet du trou du cul

This joint effort by Verlaine and Rimbaud originally appeared in *Album Zutique,* an assemblage of farcical and obscene group improvisations created by the two lovers and their circle of fellow *zutistes* in 1871 and 1872. *Sonnet du trou du cul* satirizes *l'Idole,* a sonnet sequence by the Parnassian poet Albert Mérat (1840–1909) in which each poem praises a specific bodily part of the poet's inamorata.

191

BIBLIOGRAPHY

Bouhier, Jean. *Verlaine et l'Amour.* Périgueux: Pierre Fanlac, 1946.

D'Eaubonne, Françoise. *Verlaine et Rimbaud ou la fausse évasion.* Paris: Albin Michel, 1960.

Esnault, Gaston. *Dictionnaire des Argots.* Paris: Librairie Larousse, 1965.

Farmer, John S. *Vocabula Amatoria. French-English Dictionary of Erotica.* New Hyde Park, New York: University Books, 1966.

Rowse, A. L. *Homosexuals in History.* New York: Macmillan, 1977.

Verlaine, Paul. *Confessions of a Poet,* translated by Ruth S. Wolf and Joanna Richardson, preface by Martin L. Wolf. New York: Philosophical Library, 1950.